# EARLY
# HUMANS

Flint dagger, Stone Age, c. 2000 B.C.

Flint fire starter and iron pyrites, Stone Age

Coins, Iron Age, c. 50 B.C. - A.D. 50

Digging stick (Stone Age weight with modern shaft)

Pottery beaker, c. 2200 B.C.

Terret ring, Iron Age, c. 150 B.C. - A.D. 50

Sword, late Bronze Age, c. 950 B.C.

Pottery sherd, c. 4000 B.C.

Peruvian mummified hand

Sage

EYEWITNESS BOOKS

Almonds

# EARLY HUMANS

Comb, Amazon rain forest

Fire and firestones

Arrows, as
used c. 6000 B.C.

Flint handaxe, Stone Age,
c. 200,000 B.C.

DORLING KINDERSLEY EDUCATION

London • New York • Stuttgart

Antler harpoon point

Antler comb for preparing animal hides

**A DORLING KINDERSLEY BOOK**

**Project editor** Phil Wilkinson
**Art editor** Miranda Kennedy
**Managing editor** Vicky Davenport
**Managing art editor** Jane Owen
**Special photography** Dave King
**Editorial Consultant** Nick Merriman

This is a Dorling Kindersley Education edition, 1993

This Eyewitness Book has been
conceived by Dorling Kindersley Limited
and Editions Gallimard

Manufactured in Singapore

0 9 8 7 6 5 4 3 2 1

**Library of Congress Cataloging in Publication Data**
Merriman, Nick
Early humans / written by Nick Merriman;
photography by Dave King
p. cm. – (Eyewitness Books)
Includes index
Summary: Text and photographs present a description of early humans:
their origins; their tools and weapons; how they hunted and foraged
for food; and the role of family life, money, religion, and magic.
1. Man, Prehistoric - Juvenile literature.
2. Civilization, Ancient - Juvenile literature.
[1. Man, Prehistoric. 2. Civilization, Ancient.]
I. King, Dave, ill. II. Title. III. Series
GN744.M46 1989 930.1-dc19 88-13431
ISBN 0-394-82257-9 (trade edition)
ISBN 0-394-92257-3 (lib. bdg.)
ISBN 0-7516-5110-9 (school edition)

Soay sheep's wool on spindle

Flint arrowheads, c. 2000 B.C.

Iron Age bronze bracelet, c. 50 B.C.

Plumed comb, Papua New Guinea

# Contents

Iron Age pin for fastening clothes, 800-700 B.C.

# Man or ape?

IN AFRICA around ten million years ago, the climate was slowly changing and grassland was replacing dense forest cover. To make use of this new environment, the early apes started to spend more time on the ground. They foraged for plants and scavenged the remains of animals, and this encouraged cooperation, communication, and increased intelligence. Some of them also learned to stand upright, enabling them to look over tall grass, and leaving their hands free for other tasks. Gradually, over a period of several million years, the human tribe, known as the *Hominini*, evolved in this way. Members of the *Hominini* are distinguished from their more apelike ancestors by their bigger brains, upright walking, and different teeth. The first groups to show these features are called australopithecines ("southern apes"), and were present from four to one million years ago.

**OUT OF AFRICA**
Australopithecines have been found only in E. and S. Africa. It is not clear whether humans first evolved in the area, or whether the fossils are just best preserved there.

The smallest species of australopithecine, shown here with a modern woman, was the size of an upright chimpanzee. Other species were as tall as we are.

**EARLY BIRD**
The lesser flamingo frequented shallow lakes in East Africa at the time of the earliest hominines.

**ARMS AND HANDS**
Lucy walked upright, so her hands were freer than those of apes. She did not make tools, but probably used convenient stones for some tasks.

**IN THE GRASSLANDS**
This is a reconstruction of a scene at Laetoli in East Africa about 3.75 million years ago. The region was covered by tropical grassland with lakes and a few shady trees. Early hominines foraged for food and walked upright so that they could see over the tall grass.

**FOOTPRINTS IN THE ASH**
In 1976, the footprints of two australo-pithecines, an adult and a child walking side by side, were found on this site. They had walked over freshly laid volcanic ash which had then hardened.

**"LUCY"**
In 1974, the oldest and most complete australopithecine skeleton found so far was excavated (dug up) in Ethiopia (East Africa). It was named "Lucy," after the Beatles' song "Lucy in the Sky with Diamonds," which was playing in the excavators' camp at the time.

**OLDEST SKULL**
The australopithecines had a rather apelike head, with a low forehead, a large eyebrow ridge, a flat nose, and a jutting jaw. However, their muzzles were much shorter than those of the apes and their teeth were arranged differently. This, and a number of other factors, makes them closer to humans than apes.

**GROWING BRAIN**
Australopithecines' brains, at 450-500 cc in volume, were little bigger than those of gorillas, but in terms of brain-to-body ratio, they are midway between apes and humans.

Brain size of a robust australopithecine, one of the larger species

Modern humans have a brain capacity of around 1400 cc. The brain-to-body ratio is high, and the forebrain, the seat of reason, is exceptionally large.

*Low, flattened forehead*

*Large brow ridge*

**POWERFUL JAW**
The australo-pithecine jaw was more like a human's than an ape's, but was far more powerful than ours and held bigger teeth.

## Standing

The comparisons below between human and gorilla bones show how we can tell whether they walked upright or on all fours.

**HUMAN NECK**
The human head is balanced on the top of the backbone.

**GORILLA NECK**
The backbone of a gorilla meets its head at an angle.

Forty percent of Lucy's bones were recovered.

**HISTORIC MEETING**
Two of the great names in the study of early hominines meet to discuss problems. Raymond Dart (left) found the first australopithecine in 1924. Richard Leakey (right) continues the research of his father and mother in East Africa (p. 10).

**HUMAN AND GORILLA FEET**
The gorilla's big toe sticks out at an angle and is used for grasping. In humans, the big toe is aligned with the others.

**HUMAN AND GORILLA HIPS**
Humans have a broad, short pelvis for upright walking; gorillas have a long, narrow pelvis.

7

# Prehistoric food

ALTHOUGH WE DO NOT KNOW exactly what the earliest people ate, prehistoric people clearly had a very close relationship with the animals and plants around them. Through thousands of years of experience they came to know which animals to hunt, which plants they could eat, and which plants could be used to treat illnesses. Much of this knowledge has now been lost. The prehistoric diet was much more varied than our modern diet. It even included many plants that we think of as weeds. After people started to grow corn (pp. 30-31), nutritious wild foods were still eaten. These foods could only be preserved for a short time by drying or salting, so the seasons had a strong effect on what was eaten. Another difference from our diet was that there were few sweeteners, except for honey.

**NETTLES**
The young leaves of nettles were made into a soup. Nettle juice was used in cheese making.

Rue

Catmint

**MEDICINE**
As well as being nutritious, many plants have medicinal properties that have been put to use for thousands of years. The leaves of rue were used for headaches; catmint was an ancient cold cure.

Wheat grains

An imaginative reconstruction of Stone Age hunter-gatherers preparing and cooking food

Dandelion leaves

Sunflower seeds

**SALAD DAYS**
Although now thought of as weeds, dandelion leaves were a regular salad food in prehistoric times.

Hazelnuts

Juniper berries

Almonds

Hazel twig

**FROM THE WOODS**
Woodlands yielded an abundant supply of wild nuts and berries, which are excellent sources of nutrition and can easily be stored. Hazelnuts in particular seem to have been stored for the winter, and fruit could be preserved in the form of jam. In the Near East, wheat grains were first collected wild, and then cultivated. Juniper berries made a tasty spice.

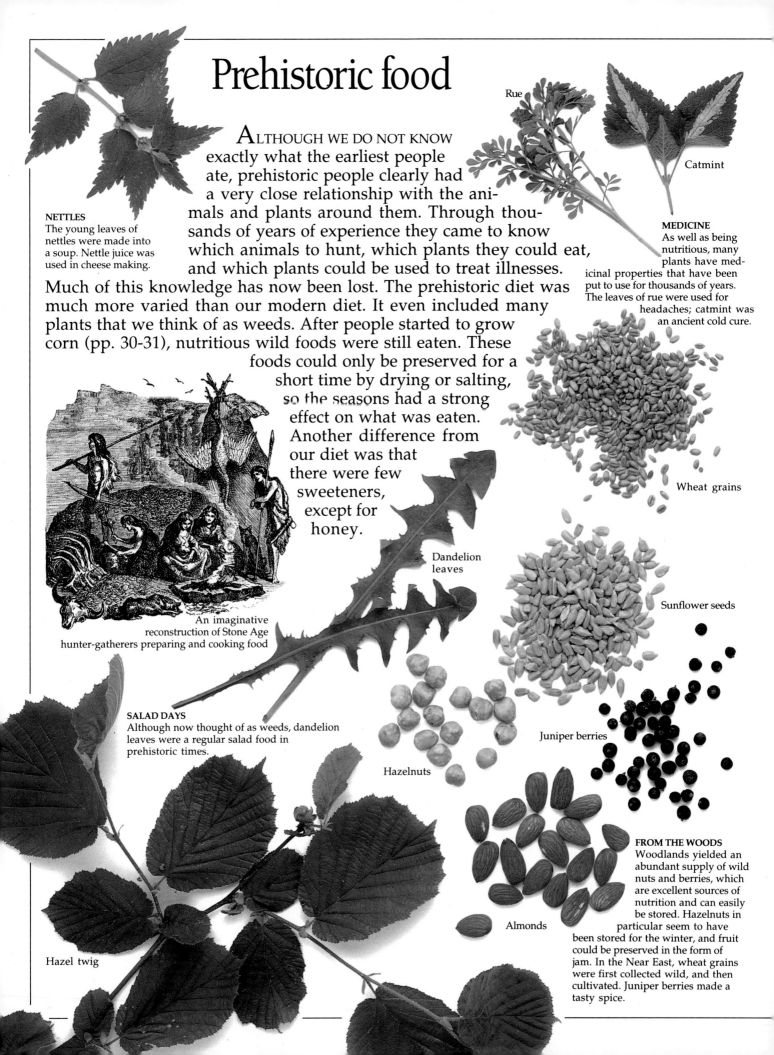

**FOODS FOR THE FAMILY**
As far as we know from recent societies, prehistoric hunter-gatherers benefited from a very broad diet, and each member of the family played his or her part in providing food. The men hunted wild animals, such as the stag shown here. The bulk of the food, however, was often gathered by the women and children. This consisted of such items as plants, eggs, nuts, and perhaps fish.

Quails' eggs

**FRUIT**
Fruit was an important food for early Mediterranean peoples. As well as being a rich source of nutrition, it could be dried and stored. Grapes could also be made into wine.

Figs

Dates

**SALMON**
From at least 10,000 B.C., people used large spears to catch salmon in the rivers of Europe.

Fenugreek

**SPICE OF LIFE**
Besides salt, which was used more to preserve food than to flavor it, a variety of seasonings and spices have a long history. Some, such as coriander, were also prized because they are good for the digestive system.

Coriander

Black cumin

Mustard

Peppercorns

Seals were good food sources for northern peoples.

Basil

**HUNTING**
This cave painting shows men hunting giant elk.

Mint

Sage

**COOKING MEAT**
This is a reconstruction of one ancient method of cooking meat. The meat was wrapped in a piece of leather and secured with a twig. This was put into a pot of water brought to boiling point by dropping in red-hot stones which had been heated in a fire (pp. 16-17). The more usual method of cooking meat was by putting it on a spit and grilling or roasting it over the glowing embers of a fire. Roasting was also done in a pit lined with heated stones.

**HERBS**
In prehistoric times, as now, herbs were often gathered to flavor food.

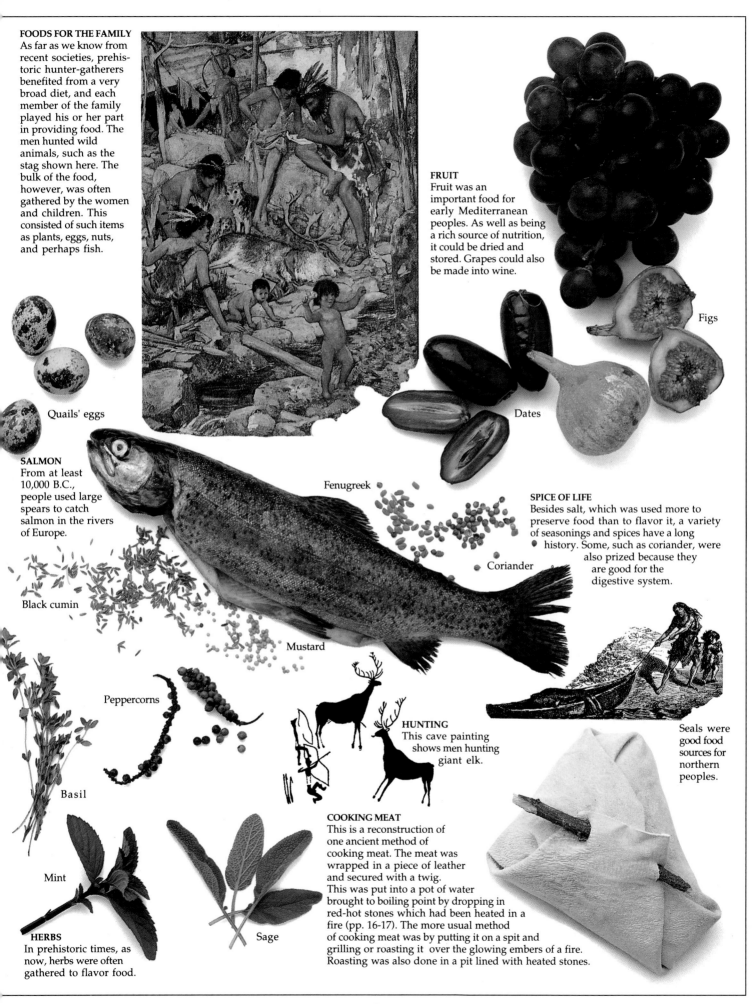

# The toolmakers

ABOUT TWO MILLION YEARS AGO one australopithecine species evolved into the other member of the human tribe, *Homo*. Compared with australopithecus, *Homo* had a bigger brain, a more human-looking face, and hip bones that were better adapted both to walking upright and to giving birth to babies with large heads. The earliest species of the genus *Homo* could make tools and was therefore named *Homo habilis* ("handy man"). Toolmaking involves using memory, planning ahead, and working out abstract problems; it marks the beginning of our use of culture to help us to adapt to our surroundings - a uniquely human ability. The habilines probably also used some primitive form of communication to pass on knowledge. They seem to have used their tools to cut meat and smash open bones for marrow. They may have hunted animals, but it is more likely that they scavenged carcasses (bodies of dead animals), and that plants were still their major source of food. There is evidence that they also made small, round huts to shelter in - the earliest buildings in the world. They lived in East Africa, and related groups may have lived in South Africa and Southeast Asia.

**PEBBLE TOOL**
There is a great difference between using tools and manufacturing them. Chimpanzees may select certain items and change them for use as tools, but humans are the only animals to use one set of tools to make other tools. This pebble tool comes from Olduvai Gorge in Tanzania (East Africa).

## The Piltdown forgery

Earlier this century, scientists were looking for a "missing link" between humans and apes. Between 1912 and 1915 amateur archaeologist Charles Dawson, and later Sir Arthur Smith Woodward of the British Museum, found a human skull with an ape's jaw in a gravel pit at Piltdown, England, together with bones of extinct animals. For years "Piltdown man" was accepted until 1953, when it was shown to be an elaborate forgery.
Who carried out the hoax is still uncertain.

**THE LEAKEY FAMILY**
The Leakey family has been involved in research in East Africa for nearly sixty years. In 1960, years of patient work paid off for Louis Leakey and his wife, Mary, when they found and named the first *Homo habilis*. Their son, Richard, pictured here, has continued their work in Ethiopia, finding many more hominine remains.

This old drawing of an orangutan stresses its human-like characteristics.

This is how it was thought the fragments of the skull fitted together.

Orangutan skull

**PILTDOWN RECONSTRUCTION**
So eager were scientists to find a missing link that many accepted the genuineness of Piltdown man immediately, and a number of reconstructions such as this one were soon made.

Sir Arthur Smith Woodward of the British Museum.

**BRAIN SIZES**
The brain of the habilines (650-800 cc) was larger than that of the australopithecines. This development happened at the same time that the habilines gained the ability to make tools, although their brain was still only half the size of a modern human brain.

Australopithecine brain

Habiline brain

Modern human brain

**SIZE AND SHAPE**
Comparisons between *Homo habilis* and modern people show that the habilines were smaller (about 4 ft 6 ins [1.5 m] tall), and almost certainly much hairier. Their feet seem to have been fully adapted for upright walking, like our own.

**THE SKULL**
*Homo habilis* had a more rounded head than the australopithecines, and a face that was smaller, longer, and narrower. The jaw was lighter, the teeth were slightly smaller, and the curve of the tooth row was more like a human's. This is a cast of a skull from Olduvai Gorge.

**AT HOME WITH THE HABILINES**
This reconstruction of a scene about 1.8 million years ago is based on excavations at Olduvai Gorge in Tanzania. The camp has been carefully placed near a lake where animals gather. In the foreground a group of habilines are constructing a shelter of branches kept in place by stones. Stone tools are being manufactured, and bones from meat scavenged from carcasses lie scattered about. In the background another group is about to kill an old giant African buffalo.

11

# Flintworking

THE FIRST TOOL-MAKING HUMAN, *Homo habilis*, made simple pebble tools from various types of rock (pp. 10-11). Later, in Europe, people found that flint was the most suitable material, and flint tools half a million years old have been found. Flint's most useful property is that regular flakes come off when it is chipped. The angle and size of the flakes can be controlled by careful chipping, and so a variety of sizes and shapes can be made. Like glass, flint takes a very sharp edge which can be resharpened by further flaking when it becomes blunt. Flint is widespread and abundant, though in many cases it has to be mined from the chalk in which it occurs. The earliest tools were made by removing flakes from a core of flint until the required shape was left. Most handaxes were made in this way. Later on, the flakes themselves were used to make finer tools and weapons, like knives and arrowheads.

**FIRST IN ENGLAND**
This handaxe is about a quarter of a million years old. It comes from Swanscombe, one of the oldest sites in England, where the earliest British human skull has been found.

*Rounded end used as hammer head*

*Flat striking platform*

**CORE**
In the earliest tools the core itself formed the tool. Later the flakes were used.

**HAMMERSTONE**
A pebble hammer like this was the simplest tool used for flintworking. The unworked flint was struck with the hammer, and large, thick flakes came away.

*Flint flake*

*Flint flake*

**2 REMOVING FLAKES**
A stone hammer was used to strike a sharp blow along the edge of the rough-cut flint. This removed a large chip from the underside.

**ANTLER HAMMER**
A light bone or antler hammer was used for chipping off smaller, thinner pieces of flint.

**1 SHAPING THE CORE**
The first step in flintworking was to select a piece of flint and to start trimming it to a rough shape.

**3 FINISHING**
The axe was trimmed by striking it along its edge with a bone hammer.

**FLINT FLAKES**
Long, thin blades such as these are made by preparing a flat platform on a core and striking the outside rim vertically with a bone hammer.

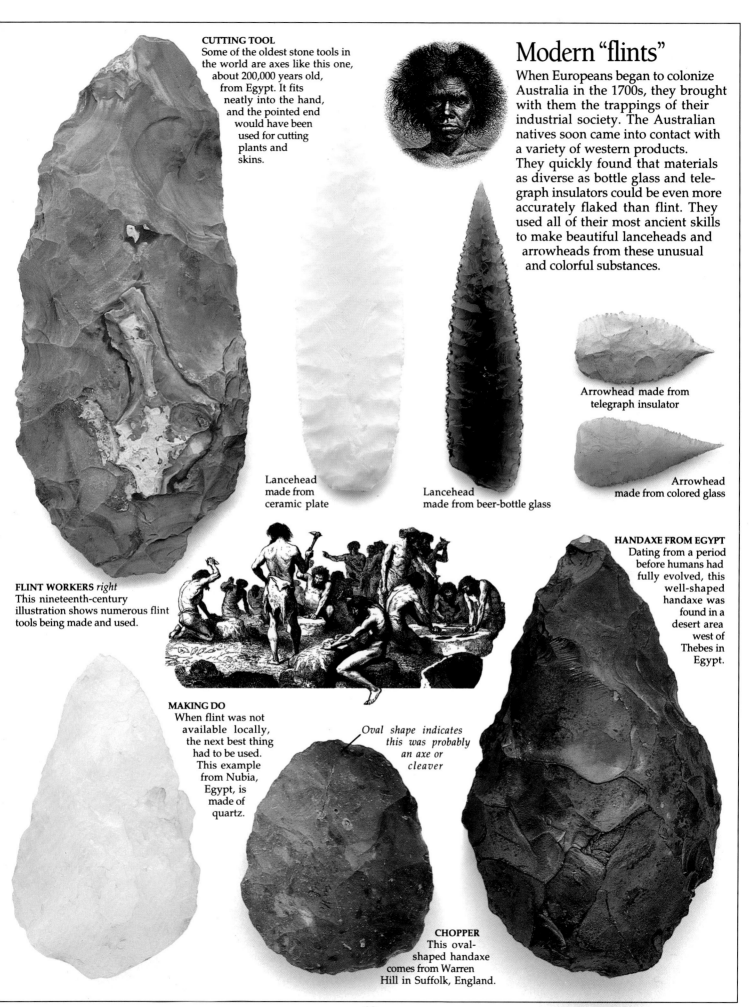

**CUTTING TOOL**
Some of the oldest stone tools in the world are axes like this one, about 200,000 years old, from Egypt. It fits neatly into the hand, and the pointed end would have been used for cutting plants and skins.

# Modern "flints"

When Europeans began to colonize Australia in the 1700s, they brought with them the trappings of their industrial society. The Australian natives soon came into contact with a variety of western products. They quickly found that materials as diverse as bottle glass and telegraph insulators could be even more accurately flaked than flint. They used all of their most ancient skills to make beautiful lanceheads and arrowheads from these unusual and colorful substances.

Arrowhead made from telegraph insulator

Lancehead made from ceramic plate

Lancehead made from beer-bottle glass

Arrowhead made from colored glass

**FLINT WORKERS** *right*
This nineteenth-century illustration shows numerous flint tools being made and used.

**HANDAXE FROM EGYPT**
Dating from a period before humans had fully evolved, this well-shaped handaxe was found in a desert area west of Thebes in Egypt.

**MAKING DO**
When flint was not available locally, the next best thing had to be used. This example from Nubia, Egypt, is made of quartz.

*Oval shape indicates this was probably an axe or cleaver*

**CHOPPER**
This oval-shaped handaxe comes from Warren Hill in Suffolk, England.

# Moving northwards

Between about 1.6 million and 200,000 years ago lived the *Homo erectus* people. They had bigger brains and bodies than the habilines, and some were probably as tall and as heavy as ourselves. They were also much more advanced than the habilines - they had a more varied toolkit and knew how to use fire. Fire provided a focus for the family group, kept people warm, and could be used for cooking. In addition it kept predators away and helped in hunting - animals could be driven into traps by using fire. These skills, and the increased brain power that goes with them, enabled these people to live a much wider range of environments than their ancestors. They were probably the first people to range beyond Africa into Europe and Asia, where most of their fossils have in fact been found. In these new environments, the harshest of which would have been Ice Age Europe, *Homo erectus* gradually adapted to local conditions. Over a million years, they evolved differently in different parts of the world, but the fossils still share enough general characteristics to show they are clearly our ancestors.

**THE SPREAD OF *HOMO ERECTUS***
Although *Homo erectus* probably started life in Africa, remains have been found in places as far away as China and Java. They colonized these areas by making short outward migrations into new territory away from each generation's family base.

**WOOLLY RHINOCEROS**
*Homo erectus* survived until well into the Ice Age, when, in Europe, colder conditions came and went at intervals of several thousand years (pp. 18-19). Adapted to this climate, the woolly rhinoceros was one of the large mammals that *Homo erectus* may have hunted.

Stick held in hand

**FIRE STICKS**
The earliest hominines might have made occasional use of natural fires caused by lightning, but *Homo erectus* seems to have been the first to create and use fire deliberately. A simple wooden tool like this would have been used to start a fire.

Groove to take stick

Wooden hearth

**FIRE MAKERS**
This scene shows a band of *Homo erectus* people in front of the cave they are using for shelter. On the right a male is starting to make a handaxe by removing flakes from a flint core with a hammerstone (p. 12). The female next to him is kindling a fire in a hearth surrounded by stones to shelter it from the wind. The people in the background are using handaxes to butcher a large mammal they have hunted. The meat will then be cooked over the open fire.

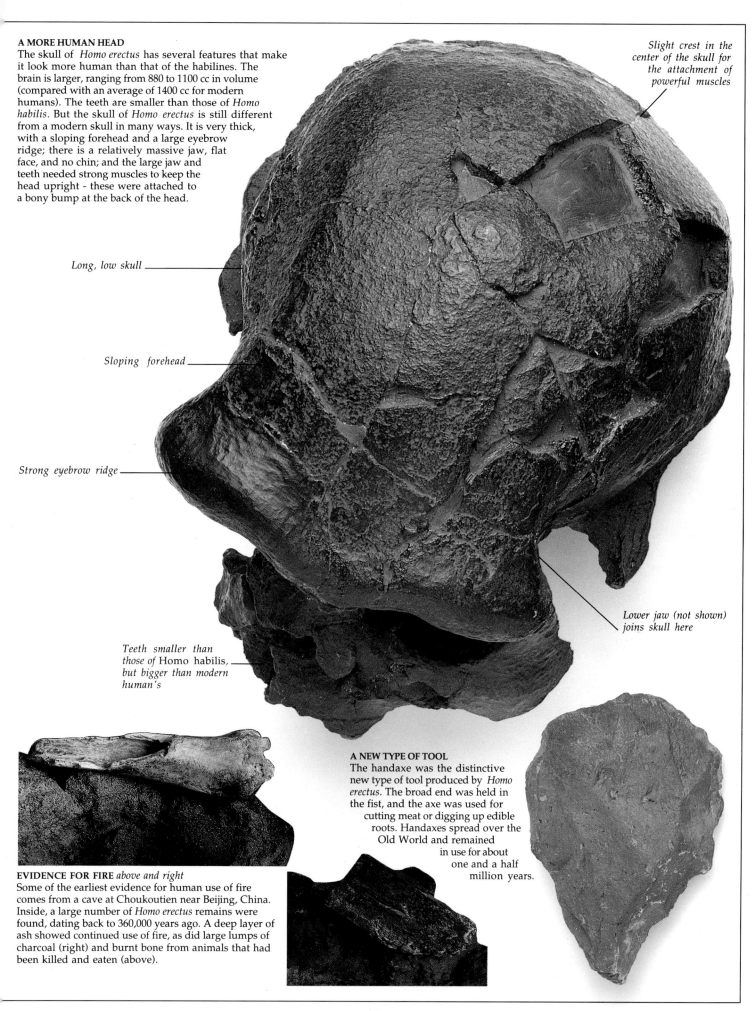

**A MORE HUMAN HEAD**
The skull of *Homo erectus* has several features that make it look more human than that of the habilines. The brain is larger, ranging from 880 to 1100 cc in volume (compared with an average of 1400 cc for modern humans). The teeth are smaller than those of *Homo habilis*. But the skull of *Homo erectus* is still different from a modern skull in many ways. It is very thick, with a sloping forehead and a large eyebrow ridge; there is a relatively massive jaw, flat face, and no chin; and the large jaw and teeth needed strong muscles to keep the head upright - these were attached to a bony bump at the back of the head.

*Slight crest in the center of the skull for the attachment of powerful muscles*

*Long, low skull*

*Sloping forehead*

*Strong eyebrow ridge*

*Lower jaw (not shown) joins skull here*

*Teeth smaller than those of* Homo habilis, *but bigger than modern human's*

**A NEW TYPE OF TOOL**
The handaxe was the distinctive new type of tool produced by *Homo erectus*. The broad end was held in the fist, and the axe was used for cutting meat or digging up edible roots. Handaxes spread over the Old World and remained in use for about one and a half million years.

**EVIDENCE FOR FIRE** *above and right*
Some of the earliest evidence for human use of fire comes from a cave at Choukoutien near Beijing, China. Inside, a large number of *Homo erectus* remains were found, dating back to 360,000 years ago. A deep layer of ash showed continued use of fire, as did large lumps of charcoal (right) and burnt bone from animals that had been killed and eaten (above).

# The coming of fire

FIRE WAS ONE OF THE MOST IMPORTANT DISCOVERIES ever made by ancient people. It not only enabled them to keep warm when the temperature was much colder than it is today, it was also useful in keeping wild animals away, in roasting meat, and in hardening the tips of wooden spears. Before they learned to make fire, people probably used accidental fires caused by lightning. The great step forward was made when they found out how to make fire for themselves by rubbing two sticks together to create a spark. The earliest evidence we have of fire is from about a quarter of a million years ago. Because no fire-making equipment survives from this remote period, archaeologists have to rely upon studies of more recent societies around the world who probably made fire in the same way as their ancestors long, long ago.

**FIRE IN THE ICE AGE**
This is a reconstruction of fire making in a cave during one of the Ice Ages about 200,000 years ago. A simple fire drill is being rapidly rotated over a piece of dry timber.

*Wooden mouthpiece to hold drill in place*

*Wooden drill*

*Wooden drill*

*Leather bow*

*Dry straw*

*Wooden hearth*

**BOW DRILL**
On this modern model of a bow drill, the leather bow makes it easy to turn the drill fast and get enough friction and heat to start a fire.

*Holes where drill has been used*

Using a bow drill

*Wooden hearth*

**FIRE DRILL**
This simple fire drill from Akamba, Kenya, shows the basic principle of generating heat by turning the drill to create friction so the wood underneath begins to burn.

Rotating the drill

**AROUND THE HEARTH**
In the sort of fire produced by the earliest fire makers, the tinder ignited by the fire drill was added to a heap of dry grass and small sticks. Larger pieces were added once the fire was alight. A circle of large stones helped to protect it from drafts.

**TWO DRY STICKS**
In the Stone Age, before the fire drill had been perfected, fire could still be made by rubbing together two dry sticks. Brushwood was used to keep the fire going.

*Sticks would be built up as the fire started to burn*

*As the stones got hot they could be used to heat water for cooking*

**AFRICAN FIRE MAKING**
Much of our knowledge of early fire-making techniques comes from studies of early African tools such as the simple wooden drill.

# Life in the Ice Age

THE ICE AGE consisted of several alternate cold and warm periods, each lasting tens of thousands of years. During some of these periods the climate was actually warmer than it is today, and only for parts of the period was there extensive ice coverage of northern Europe. The *Homo erectus* people were the first to live in this area, probably only in the warm periods. By 250,000 years ago, people were slowly adapting to living in the cold periods, and 150,000 years later the first distinct subspecies of modern humans, *Homo sapiens neanderthalensis*, can be recognized. Neanderthals were very similar to people today, and if they were dressed in modern clothes, they would not attract any attention. They would just be slightly smaller, stockier, and heavier-featured than average. Those found in the warmer Mediterranean areas were even more modern-looking. Neanderthals show the first stirrings of humanness: they cared for the disabled, buried their dead carefully, and probably had some sort of religion. They were abruptly replaced about 35,000 years ago by fully modern people, *Homo sapiens sapiens*, who had been evolving in the meantime in the warmer climate of Africa. They colonized huge areas of the world at this time, including Europe in its final icy phase, and even Australia.

**THE ICE AGE AND THE NEANDERTHALS**
This map shows the maximum extent of the ice sheets (blue), and the land exposed by the resulting lowering of the sea level. The spread of Neanderthals over a period of 60,000 years is indicated in brown, and the red dot shows the Neander Valley in Germany, where the first fossils were found.

**HOME ON THE TUNDRA**
When *Homo sapiens sapiens* colonized the cold Russian tundra, they used methods of house-building employed by the Neanderthals. This reconstruction shows a dwelling excavated at Pushkari, consisting of sewn skins stretched over a frame of poles, weighted down by mammoth bones.

**MAMMOTH BONE HUTS**
Remarkable evidence of Neanderthal huts has been found in the Russian Ukraine. They were made of animal skins on a frame of branches or long mammoth bones, and the outsides were heavily weighted with more bones.

**THE NEANDERTHAL WARDROBE**
Neanderthals were probably the first humans to wear clothes all the time, to protect themselves from the cold. When making clothes, they would first stretch out an animal hide such as a deerskin, and then use flint tools to scrape it clean of fat and sinews. After tanning, they would sew the hide into the required shape.

**TOOLMAKING**
Neanderthal toolkits were a great improvement on those used by *Homo erectus*. They could produce a wide range of fine tools for a variety of tasks. Bone and antler were widely used, as well as flint.

**LIFE IN A COLD CLIMATE**
Neanderthals were well adapted for living in a cold climate, and their lifestyle may have been similar to some of the Inuit people's (pp. 20-21). They probably lived in extended family groups, each member of which would carry out a variety of tasks. This scene reflects the many abilities of this first truly human group.

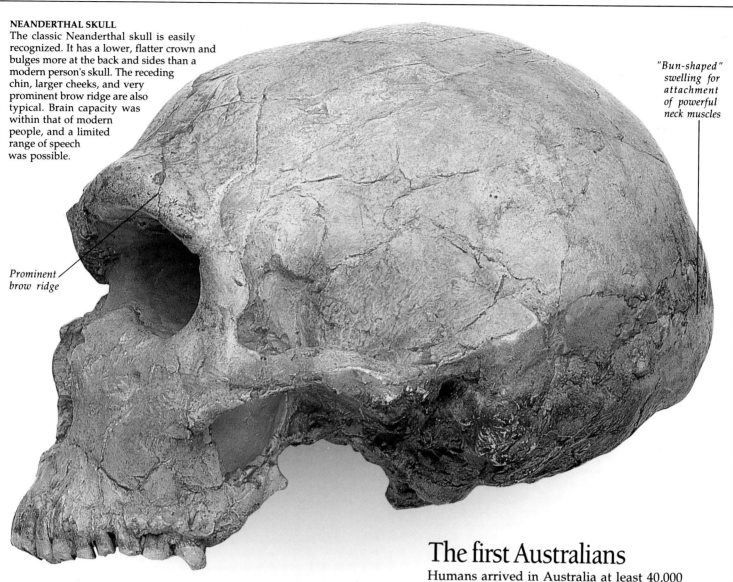

### NEANDERTHAL SKULL
The classic Neanderthal skull is easily recognized. It has a lower, flatter crown and bulges more at the back and sides than a modern person's skull. The receding chin, larger cheeks, and very prominent brow ridge are also typical. Brain capacity was within that of modern people, and a limited range of speech was possible.

*"Bun-shaped" swelling for attachment of powerful neck muscles*

*Prominent brow ridge*

### SCRAPER
By the time of the Neanderthals, people were able to make a wide variety of stone tools and weapons, using flakes struck from a prepared core (p. 12). This is a flint scraper for preparing skins.

### GROUP OF NEANDERTHALS
The prominent brow ridge and strong jaw are particularly clear features of the Neanderthal people.

## The first Australians
Humans arrived in Australia at least 40,000 years ago, possibly much earlier. The earliest human remains found are those of fully modern people, who must have come by boat or raft from Southeast Asia. Some later skulls show older traits, so a mixture of groups may have colonized the area. The Aborigines continued to live a Stone Age life until 200 years ago.

### WATERCRAFT
The first humans arriving in Australia probably traveled on a raft or in a simple canoe like this one. The sea at this time was up to 164 ft (50 m) lower, so the mainland was only about 40 miles (65 km) away.

**Australian Aborigine**

# Ice Age hunters

FEW REMAINS SURVIVE FROM THE ICE AGE (two million to 15,000 years ago) except some stone and bone objects made by the hunters of the period. We have some idea what these peoples' clothes and houses might have looked like (pp. 18-19), but we have no direct evidence of their way of life. However, by studying more recent people from a similar climate, we can learn a great deal about what life must have been like in the Ice Age. The Inuit (whom we used to call Eskimos) live along the coasts of Greenland and North America and have survived for thousands of years in a landscape where even the sea is frozen solid for much of the year. Although they have adopted many of the useful trappings of western society, until the last century the Inuit way of life must have been very close to that of hunter-fishers during the Ice Age.

**ICE FLOES**
This illustration gives an impression of the Arctic landscape, with its icebergs and snowy hills with sparse vegetation.

*Spears and harpoons*

*Waterproof clothes made of seal or walrus skin*

**IN PURSUIT OF FOOD**
Throughout their history, the Inuit have hunted different animals of sea and river. In the summer they net or spear spawning fish and hunt caribous and seals; the seals are caught either by spearing them through holes in the ice or by throwing harpoons at them from boats. They use two main types of skin-covered boat - the kayak, which is like a modern canoe but covered over on top, and the umiak, which is open-topped and much larger. Sometimes a small fleet manage to kill a whale, as shown in the bone engraving above.

**ARROW STRAIGHTENER**
Straight arrows are essential for accurate shooting. This straightener is in the form of a kneeling caribou.

*Engravings of caribou*

*Bladder float*

**INUIT ARSENAL**
Harpoons and spears are used by the Inuit for hunting from boats; arrows are for use on land.

*Wooden shaft over 6 ft (2 m) long*

### KAYAK
This model of an Inuit kayak is fully equipped with miniature spears and harpoons. Waterproof coverings surround each figure and are secured with a drawstring to keep water from getting into the kayak.

*Skin exterior*

*Protective skin covering*

### POWERFUL POINTS
These notched ivory harpoon points are attached to a line which reels out as the wounded animal tries to swim away.

### LONG-DISTANCE WEAPON
The spear works in a way similar to the harpoon, but is thrown from a greater distance.

### LYING IN WAIT
When the sea is frozen, the Inuit hunt seals through the ice. The seals have to come to holes in the ice in order to breathe, so the hunters wait until a seal appears at the surface.

*Ivory harpoon head*

### WHALER'S WEAPON
Large harpoons such as this are hurled from boats at walruses or even whales. The bladder keeps the harpoon afloat if it misses the target, so that the hunter can retrieve it.

*Skin line*

### SNOW KNIVES
These two knives were made for cutting blocks of snow for igloo making. They are richly engraved with different scenes showing animals, hunters, and houses.

*Thin viewing slits to eliminate glare*

### GOGGLES
These protect the wearer from the glare of the snow.

### BONE KNIVES
The Inuit are careful not to waste any part of the animals they hunt. Bone is used for tools and weapons. The one on the left has animal gut twined around the handle to give a better grip.

*Hunting scene*

### CARVING
The Inuit have a strong tradition of carving. Here a craftsman is engraving a piece of ivory with a knife.

# Modern humans

MOST EXPERTS BELIEVE that the subspecies to which we belong, *Homo sapiens sapiens*, evolved in Africa around 100,000 years ago. By 30,000 years ago, *sapiens* had spread to all parts of the world except the Americas, and by at least 11,000 years ago, every continent but Antarctica was populated. Interbreeding with the local peoples might have produced the different races that inhabit the world today. *Homo sapiens sapiens* developed several skills and patterns of behavior that were seen dimly among the Neanderthals. Communication through art and the spoken word became a vital part of human life; people carefully buried their dead and had some concept of religion and an afterlife; and hunting skills probably reached their peak. Later human developments - farming, civilization, huge population growth, industry, and control over nature - have occurred in the relatively short period of ten thousand years.

**PAINTED HAND**
About 20,000 years ago in a cave at Pech-Merle in France, someone produced this "negative" hand by placing his or her hand on the wall and painting over it. The hand, the part of us that makes and uses tools and is used for signaling, is a powerful symbol.

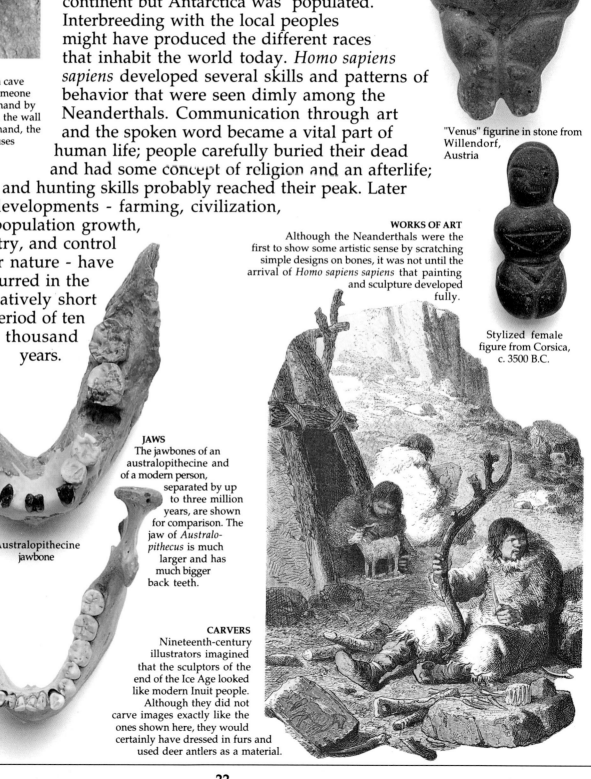

"Venus" figurine in stone from Willendorf, Austria

**WORKS OF ART**
Although the Neanderthals were the first to show some artistic sense by scratching simple designs on bones, it was not until the arrival of *Homo sapiens sapiens* that painting and sculpture developed fully.

Stylized female figure from Corsica, c. 3500 B.C.

Australopithecine jawbone

Modern human jawbone

**JAWS**
The jawbones of an australopithecine and of a modern person, separated by up to three million years, are shown for comparison. The jaw of *Australopithecus* is much larger and has much bigger back teeth.

**CARVERS**
Nineteenth-century illustrators imagined that the sculptors of the end of the Ice Age looked like modern Inuit people. Although they did not carve images exactly like the ones shown here, they would certainly have dressed in furs and used deer antlers as a material.

**FINALLY - US!**
The skull of a modern human is different from that of a Neanderthal in several important ways. First, the forehead is flat rather than sloping, and ends in only a very slight eyebrow ridge. The nose and jaws are smaller, and the teeth are more crowded together. This makes the face fairly straight rather than forward-jutting.

*More rounded braincase*

*Steep brow ridge*

*Smaller nose*

*Less jutting face*

*Point where spine joins base of skull*

*Smaller teeth*

# Evolution

The skulls below show a classic view of the evolution of humanity from the apes, as suggested by Darwin and his followers. In reality the story is far more complicated, and there are huge gaps in our knowledge. For example, we are not descended from present-day gorillas or chimpanzees, because they have been evolving too. But apes and modern people may share some ancestors. In addition, there has not been a smooth progress, but a series of fits and starts, with many species around at the same time, some surviving, others becoming extinct.

**SENSITIVE CREATURE**
In this 19th-century cartoon, the offended gorilla is pointing to Darwin and saying "That Man wants to claim my pedigree. He says he is one of my descendants."

Charles Darwin (1809-82) first publicized the idea of evolution.

Skull of primitive reptile (230-195 million years old)

Skull of mammal (54-16 million years old)

Skull of modern chimpanzee

Skull of modern man

# The first artists

THE EARLIEST WORKS OF ART were created around 30,000 years ago, during the last Ice Age. Because the making of art is unique to humankind, we can say with confidence that by this period the creators of such works were truly human. These early works of art take two main forms. The most famous are the vivid paintings of animals which cover the walls and roofs of caves, such as those at Lascaux in France and Altamira in Spain. The other, less well-known type consists of small sculptures and relief carvings of animals and female figures. These have also been found in caves, but they occur in larger numbers in open-air sites in eastern Europe.

**MASTERPIECE OF CAVE ART**
This painting is in a cave at Altamira, Spain.

*From the cave of Mas d'Azil, France*

**HORSES' HEADS**
The accuracy of these carvings shows that the artist must have observed wild horses at close quarters.

**MAMMOTH CARVING**
A skillful sculptor carved this animal's shoulder blade into a stylized mammoth with large tusks that curve around its head. Mammoths were common until the end of the Ice Age.

**IN HOT PURSUIT** *right*
The earliest artists carved pictures of the wild animals they hunted for food. This one is engraved on bone and shows a bison being followed by a human figure. It is from Laugerie Basse, France.

**HUNTER'S QUARRY**
A stag and four chamois are carved on this piece of bone. These creatures similiar to antelopes, are still found in Europe.

**GOOD-LUCK CHARM**
This old illustration shows a man carving a piece of antler to bring success in hunting.

**HORSE'S HEAD**
This engraving on bone was found in a cave at Laugerie Basse, France.

**MAKING THE COLORS** *right*
In this reconstruction, an artist is grinding up a pigment to make paint. Early artists used earth colors such as ochres, and pigments made from other naturally occurring minerals.

**PATTERNED PLAQUE**
This plaque, made from a type of stone called schist, was produced over 4,000 years after cave painting had died out, and is engraved in a quite different, abstract, geometric style. It was found in a large stone tomb at Alentjo, Portugal, and dates from the New Stone Age (c. 4000 B.C.).

**ARTISTS AT WORK**
This artist is painting the animals he is going to hunt. This activity would have formed part of his religious ritual. Light for the painters was provided by burning fat in a lamp.

Marble figurine from Melos, Greece, c. 2500-2000 B.C.

**PAINTED POTTERY**
As well as being useful, pottery can also be strikingly painted and engraved. This example is about 6,000 years old and comes from Rumania.

**BISON**
This is another painting from the famous Spanish cave at Altamira.

Found at the site of Lespugue, France

**MYSTERIOUS FIGURES**
These so-called "Venus figurines" have been found right across Europe from Spain to Russia, and date from c. 25,000-15,000 B.C. They are always faceless, and heavily pregnant. They seem to show the importance placed on reproduction and the survival of the species.

From Brno, Czechoslovakia

**THE POTTER'S ART**
The decoration on many early pots was engraved in the surface of the clay.

# Hunting and gathering

**STONE AGE HUNTERS**
Both spears and bows and arrows were used to hunt for food in the Stone Age.

FOR NINETY-NINE PERCENT of their time on earth, humans have survived by hunting animals and gathering plants for food. During the Ice Age, people in Europe were probably hunting big game such as the woolly mammoth. About 75,000 years ago people on the coast of South Africa were catching seals and penguins; and 25,000 years ago the first Australians were hunting now-extinct giant kangaroos. Throughout the prehistoric period, it is likely that most of the hunter-gatherers' food came from plants, nuts, fruits, and shellfish, because these could be gathered with little effort. Their remains do not survive as well as bones, however, so they are not often found on archaeological sites. But the discovery of flint spearheads and arrowheads suggests that early peoples had evolved quite sophisticated methods of hunting game.

*Bark "plate"*

*Blackberries*

**FRUIT AND NUTS**
Remains of these high-energy foods have been found preserved in hunters' camps from 12,000 years ago.

*Hazelnuts*

**HARPOON POINT**
This point is made of antler and is about 10,000 years old.

*Antler is easily made into harpoons like these*

**FISHING TACKLE** *above*
Found near London, this harpoon would have been used for spearing fish from a sandbank at the river's edge. It dates from c. 8000 B.C.

*Twine binding*

**SIMPLE BUT DEADLY** *above and below*
Two halves of a reproduction of a middle Stone Age arrow. The bow and arrow were developed to hunt the shy forest animals from a distance.

*Flight of duck feathers*

*Fire-hardened wooden point*

*Reproduction wooden shaft*

**FLINT ARROW**
Arrows like this were used about 8,000 years ago. The head was stuck in place with birch resin glue.

*Flints glued in groove cut in shaft*

*Reproduction shaft*

26

**Antler sleeve**

**Alternative method of binding**

*Wedge to prevent movement*

**DUAL-PURPOSE TOOL**
This adze head is fitted into an antler sleeve and secured to the handle by a leather thong. It may have been used for digging up edible roots or for woodworking.

*Wooden sleeve*

*Head dates from c. 10,000-4000 B.C.*

*Perforated quartzite pebble*

**FINEST FLINTS**
In the early Bronze Age, a variety of finely worked flint arrowheads were produced. Some were shaped ornately.

Traditional shape

**SMALL FLINT ADZE**
An adze has an uneven cutting edge and is mounted with the blade at right-angles to the handle. Used to cut wood, it is usually swung down, often between the legs. This one is inserted into a wooden sleeve and secured with animal glue or resin.

**HUNTER'S PREY**
Cave paintings, some 20,000 years old, often show animals that were hunted at the time, like this deer in the Dordogne, France.

*Reproduction wooden handles*

*Iron pyrites*

*Flint fire starter*

Missing shaft

**FIRE-MAKING**
If the iron pyrites are hit with the flint, a spark is produced. On dry grass the spark can be fanned into a flame.

Incurved design

This reindeer is being butchered with a stone axe.

*Modern wooden stick*

# Hunters of the desert

IN THE KALAHARI DESERT of southern Africa live a group of people known as the San, or Bushmen, one of the few peoples who still live by hunting animals and gathering wild plants. Although they inhabit a very different environment from the Inuit hunters (pp. 20-21), their way of life can also help us to understand hunter-gatherers of the past. As usual among hunter-gatherer peoples, the San women gather the edible roots and nuts that provide the bulk of the diet, while the men add to the food supply by hunting animals. Antelope are a favorite target for the San bowmen, and smaller animals are trapped with nooses and snares.

Bone

Hoof

Vertebrae

Arrow

Horn

**DIVINING KIT**
This contains charms made from parts of antelope, including the horn, hoof, and foot bones. The hunter uses them to "divine" when to hunt.

Wooden quiver

**READY FOR THE CHASE**
Some African peoples use large, metal-tipped spears for hunting. These are more powerful than the San's small bow.

Bow is about 2 ft (60 cm) long

Spare arrow tip

Wooden shaft without tip

Poison quill-tipped arrow

Poison quill-tipped arrow

Metal-tipped arrow

**STRAIGHTENER**
This grooved stone is heated and pressed along a fresh reed to form a straight arrowshaft.

**THE POWER OF POISON**
Some of these arrows have metal tips, but many have detachable poison quill tips. The poison, made from beetle larvae, works slowly - hunters often have to follow the animals until they die.

Slate tip    Quartz tip    Iron tip    Bone tip

Metal-tipped arrow

Metal-tipped arrow

**METAL-TIPPED SPEAR**
The San sometimes use spears instead of bows for hunting larger animals, and also for fighting.

Gazelle

Snare wound around twig

Noose of twine

*Straps made from animal's legs*

**SNARES AND NOOSES**
This selection of snares and nooses is used for trapping small animals.

**CARRYING BAG**
This bag is used for carrying equipment such as snares, and the small animals caught in them.

**ON THE RETREAT**
Like the Bushmen, Zulu warriors of southeast Africa sometimes used their long metal spears for fighting.

**MINIATURE BOW**
With a small bow, the poison tips of the arrows have to do most of the work of killing the animal.

**WEAPONS AT THE READY**
This large leather bag is slung over the hunter's shoulder to carry his bow and the wooden quiver with its arrows. The legs of the animal are tied together to form the straps.

# Tilling the soil

HUMANITY'S GREATEST-EVER ADVANCEMENT, farming first began in the Near East around 10,000 B.C. and spread throughout Europe during the next six thousand years. It also developed independently in America, the Far East, and other areas of the world. The ability to grow plants and raise animals meant that people could control their sources of food rather than rely only on hunting and gathering. Farming enabled people to stay in one place all year round and to fill a greater number of mouths. As a result the population increased and towns began to develop.

*Flint cutting-edge (c. 4000-2300 B.C.) in modern handle*

*Bronze cutting-edge*

*Reproduction handle*

*Iron cutting-edge*

**THRESHING**
This Iron Age farmer is beating corn to remove the grains.

Sheaf of corn

**CLEARING THE GROUND**
In the forested areas of Europe, pioneer farmers used axes like this one to clear huge areas of land for their fields.

**THE FIRST HARVEST**
This variety, Einkorn wheat, grows wild in Turkey and Iran, where it was first cultivated.

**BACKBREAKING TASK**
Cereal crops were harvested with sickles until the coming of the combine harvester in the early part of this century. These three examples represent the three "ages" of prehistory - stone, bronze, and iron.

*Leather binding*

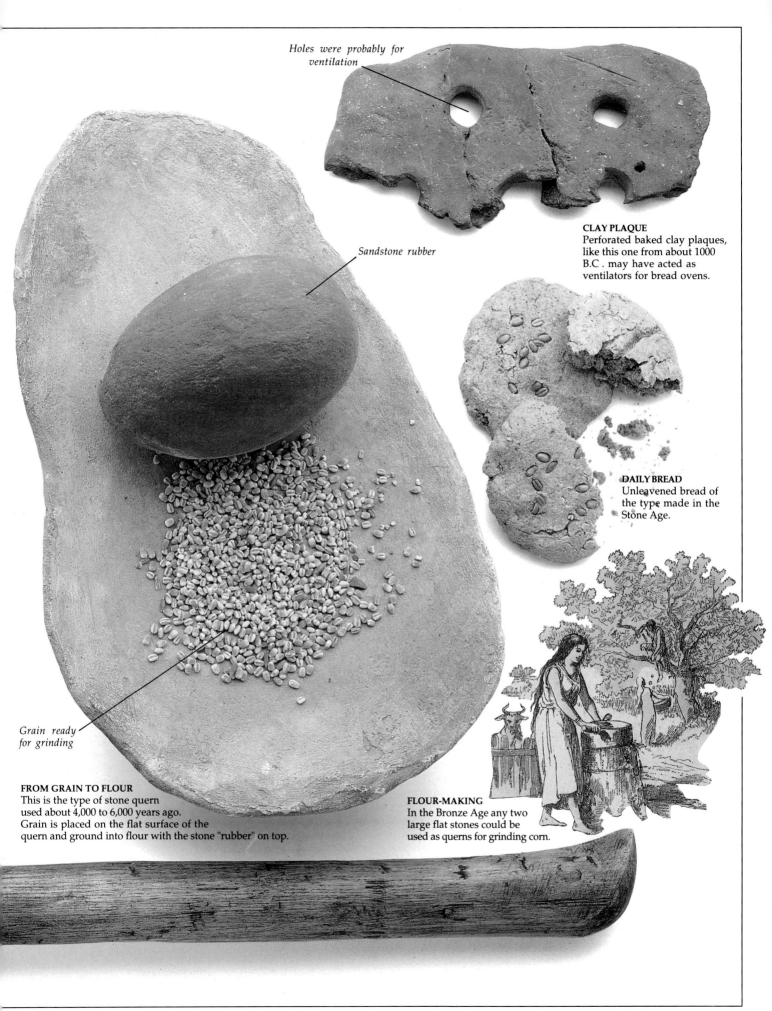

Holes were probably for ventilation

**CLAY PLAQUE**
Perforated baked clay plaques, like this one from about 1000 B.C . may have acted as ventilators for bread ovens.

Sandstone rubber

**DAILY BREAD**
Unleavened bread of the type made in the Stone Age.

Grain ready for grinding

**FROM GRAIN TO FLOUR**
This is the type of stone quern used about 4,000 to 6,000 years ago. Grain is placed on the flat surface of the quern and ground into flour with the stone "rubber" on top.

**FLOUR-MAKING**
In the Bronze Age any two large flat stones could be used as querns for grinding corn.

# Clothing and fabrics

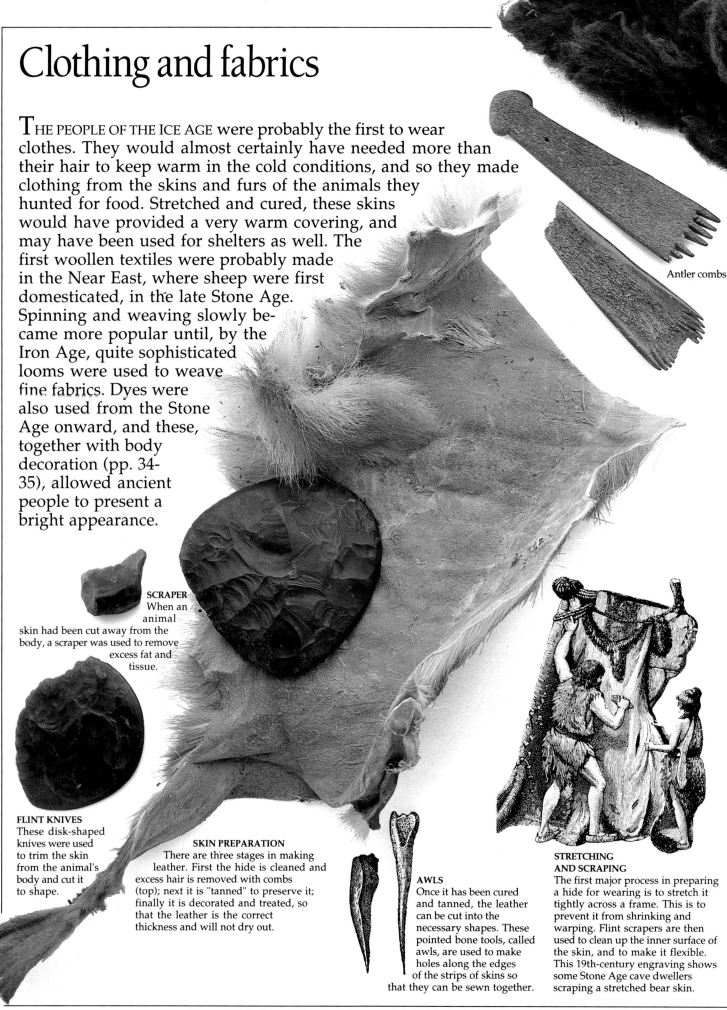

THE PEOPLE OF THE ICE AGE were probably the first to wear clothes. They would almost certainly have needed more than their hair to keep warm in the cold conditions, and so they made clothing from the skins and furs of the animals they hunted for food. Stretched and cured, these skins would have provided a very warm covering, and may have been used for shelters as well. The first woollen textiles were probably made in the Near East, where sheep were first domesticated, in the late Stone Age. Spinning and weaving slowly became more popular until, by the Iron Age, quite sophisticated looms were used to weave fine fabrics. Dyes were also used from the Stone Age onward, and these, together with body decoration (pp. 34-35), allowed ancient people to present a bright appearance.

**Antler combs**

**SCRAPER**
When an animal skin had been cut away from the body, a scraper was used to remove excess fat and tissue.

**FLINT KNIVES**
These disk-shaped knives were used to trim the skin from the animal's body and cut it to shape.

**SKIN PREPARATION**
There are three stages in making leather. First the hide is cleaned and excess hair is removed with combs (top); next it is "tanned" to preserve it; finally it is decorated and treated, so that the leather is the correct thickness and will not dry out.

**AWLS**
Once it has been cured and tanned, the leather can be cut into the necessary shapes. These pointed bone tools, called awls, are used to make holes along the edges of the strips of skins so that they can be sewn together.

**STRETCHING AND SCRAPING**
The first major process in preparing a hide for wearing is to stretch it tightly across a frame. This is to prevent it from shrinking and warping. Flint scrapers are then used to clean up the inner surface of the skin, and to make it flexible. This 19th-century engraving shows some Stone Age cave dwellers scraping a stretched bear skin.

### RAW WOOL
In ancient times the raw wool was simply plucked off the back of the sheep when it was molting.

### SPINNING AND WEAVING
This old engraving shows two of the main processes in wool production. The woman in the foreground is spinning the raw wool on the tree into a single thread by twining it around a spindle in her left hand. The man in the background is using a loom to weave the vertical and horizontal threads.

*Spun wool*

*Spindle whorl*

### SPINDLE
The raw wool is twisted around and around the wooden spindle to make a single thread. The clay spindle whorl on the end provides a weight to help the spinning motion.

Safflower yellow

Safflower red

### WOOL DYES
The safflower, or dyer's thistle, has been used since 2000 B.C.

### ANCIENT WOOL
This wool comes from a species of wild sheep which now lives only on the Isle of Soay in the Hebrides islands, off Scotland. It gives us a good idea of what ancient wool looked like. The brown color is quite natural. This wool was spun into a single thread and is now ready to be knitted or woven into a garment or a container.

Neolithic textile

*Hole for suspension*

### LOOM
The loom, first invented in the late Stone Age, made it possible to produce woven fabrics for the first time. The frame stretches the vertical woollen threads, and a shuttle is used to weave the horizontal threads in between them.

Recent American backstrap loom

Bone shuttle

Clay loomweight for stretching threads

# Skin deep

IN THE PAST, most people decorated their bodies much more than we do in the West today. Tomb paintings, sculptures, and preserved bodies give us some idea of the kinds of ornament used by peoples of the past, and we can glean more information from looking at recent non-Western cultures. The types of decoration used range from tattooing and body-painting to elaborate hairstyling and the wearing of jewelry by both men and women.

**THE POWER OF PAINTING**
Native American medicine men sometimes used elaborate body painting for ceremonies.

**SEEING RED**
Red pigment (rouge), kept in this box from southern New Guinea, may be applied just to the face or all over the body.

**UNLIKELY PERFUME**
Ambergris comes from the intestines of sperm whales. It is strong-smelling and was used as a basis for scents in the islands of the South Pacific.

**FOR BAD BREATH**
The resin from a type of spruce tree, frankincense was used to sweeten the breath.

Seed pods

**FACE PAINT**
This lump of red face paint and the seed pods from which it was made come from Gran Chaco, South America.

Ground pigments

Spoon and spatula for preparing kohl for use as makeup

**HAIR COMB**
People of the Amazon rain forest used decorated combs like this.

**EYE MAKEUP**
These blocks were ground into a powder called kohl. Kohl was used for darkening the skin around the eyes.

**BLACK AND BEAUTIFUL**
This carved coconut contains noti, a mixture for blackening the teeth. It comes from the Solomon Islands.

### LEOPARD
As well as being dangerous animals, predators such as leopards were seen in some societies as sources of strength.

### LEOPARD-CLAW NECKLACE
As well as being decorative, this necklace from Nigeria would have been thought to have a magical power.

*Feathers have long been a popular form of adornment among many cultures*

*Leopard's claw*

### DRESSED TO KILL
A hunter of 10,000 years ago wearing a necklace of animal teeth and several armlets.

### INSECT NECKLACE
Made from the bodies of over a hundred hornets, this necklace is from the Naga Hills, Burma.

*Each section is made up of one hornet's body*

Hornet

### PLUMED COMB
This simple bone comb, decorated with feathers, was collected from Papua New Guinea during the last century.

### PENDANT
This pendant was worn by Aborigines in central Australia.

African tribesman with feathered headdress

# Magic

AMONG SMALL-SCALE, non-scientific societies, magic and witchcraft are an important part of everyday life. In such a world it is natural to believe that misfortunes such as illness and accidents are caused by powers which take the form of spirits. It is also understandable that people believe that they must consult the spirits in order to find out why some evil has occurred, and what can be done to remedy it. Sometimes it is the job of a particular person - known as a shaman, diviner, or witch doctor - to do this. Usually some sort of offering will need to be made or a ritual performed. Charms are also often worn to protect the wearer from evil. It is likely that the very earliest humans practiced magic, using it to tell them the best times and places to hunt and the best ways to cure illnesses, but little evidence survives. Most of the objects shown here are therefore from recent societies.

**THE DEVIL'S DANCE**
This shaman is performing the devil's dance, a religious ceremony of the west coast of Africa. Elaborate costumes, made to look like animals or birds, are a common feature of such ceremonies.

**FOR FERTILITY**
These objects, made of a substance called faience, are Egyptian fertility symbols.

This African shaman is using a snake and some bones to foretell the future.

*Cowrie shells*

**CHARMS** *right and below*
In ancient societies it was a common practice to wear charms (sometimes called amulets) to guard against harm. These took many shapes, but were often worn around the wrist, like the charm bracelets of today.

Cowrie-shell charm from the Mojave-Apache Indians

Bead bracelet from northern India

**SACRED BUNDLE**
This leather bundle from Uganda (East Africa) is covered with cowrie shells. It originally contained various sacred objects used by a diviner.

**POWERFUL POPPY**
The narcotic effects of opium poppy seeds have been known for thousands of years. In some societies witch doctors used drugs like this to produce trances.

*Piece of wood that was floated on the water in the divining bowl*

**BELLS**
In many cases divining is done in a trance-like state along with music and dancing. Drums are used, and bells, like these goat bells from Tanzania, are sometimes rung continuously.

**DIVINING BOWL**
Divining bowls help people learn the causes of misfortune. This one from Tanzania was filled with water. Objects were then floated on the surface and the shaman figured out the meaning of their movements.

*Nutshells*

A huge stilt-walking figure in the Apono giant dance

**FOR GOOD HEALTH**
This little red figure is made up of a combination of wood, bone, leather, cloth, and nuts. It was used among the Nte'va people of central Africa to "watch one's body" - in other words, to protect a person from illness.

**DIRECT LINE TO THE SPIRITS**
Diviners communicate with a spirit in different ways. Some read messages, some become possessed by the spirit itself, and some speak directly to it through sacred objects like this antelope horn from central Africa.

**FISH CHARM**
This amulet was worn around the neck as a charm against evil spirits. It was collected in Papua New Guinea and is in the form of a local snapping fish inside a basket.

# Death and burial

Since the first Neanderthal burials about 40,000 years ago (see page 18), most people have disposed of their dead formally - by burial, cremation, or mummification. For most, death was not the end of their existence, but one stage in a journey. Death has often been seen as the time when the spirit leaves the body to live elsewhere - in heaven, in the landscape, in a tomb, or simply in the household. So in ancient societies, as now, death was looked on as an important stage in a person's existence and was marked with ceremonies. The treatment of the dead varied greatly from society to society, and was often a complicated procedure. In some ancient societies, a funeral pyre was built and the dead person cremated with sacrificial victims. The bones might then be housed in a burial chamber with offerings to accompany the individual in the afterlife. Because such burials were performed deliberately, they are often very well preserved. By studying burial remains, archaeologists can tell quite a lot about the treatment of the dead in a particular ancient society, and learn something about the living society too.

**AN EARLY BURIAL**
This reconstruction shows the burial of a woman in front of a cave at Les Eyzies, France. The site dates from around 12,000-9000 B.C.

The entrance to a chambered tomb, the Cairn of Dowth, Ireland

**THE PYRAMIDS**
This cemetery in Egypt, containing some of the most famous tombs in the world, was built between 2700 and 2500 B.C. The three largest pyramids contained the pharaohs Khufu, Khafra, and Menkaura.

**HOUSES OF THE DEAD**
"Megaliths" is the name given to a group of monuments consisting of huge slabs of stone. Some of them seem never to have housed human remains, but were simply monuments, while others contained the remains of dozens of jumbled-up skeletons. These examples are around five thousand years old.

Mummy pits are visible in the foreground

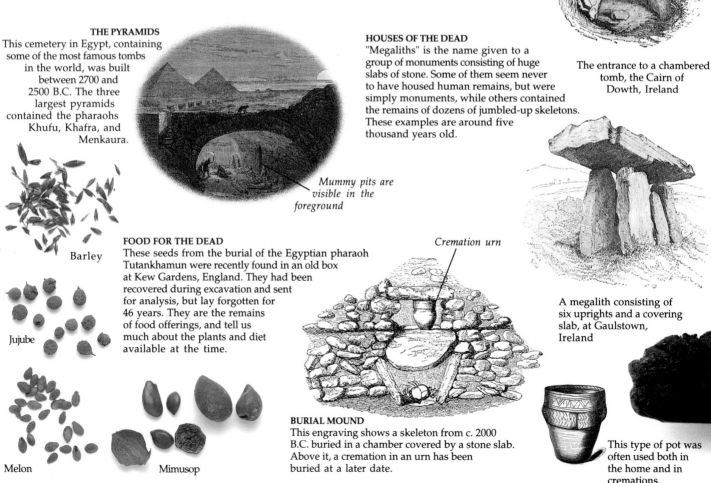

Barley

**FOOD FOR THE DEAD**
These seeds from the burial of the Egyptian pharaoh Tutankhamun were recently found in an old box at Kew Gardens, England. They had been recovered during excavation and sent for analysis, but lay forgotten for 46 years. They are the remains of food offerings, and tell us much about the plants and diet available at the time.

Jujube

Melon

Mimusop

Cremation urn

A megalith consisting of six uprights and a covering slab, at Gaulstown, Ireland

**BURIAL MOUND**
This engraving shows a skeleton from c. 2000 B.C. buried in a chamber covered by a stone slab. Above it, a cremation in an urn has been buried at a later date.

This type of pot was often used both in the home and in cremations.

# Mummification

Although we usually associate mummies with the Egyptians, they also occur in other areas of the world. In certain parts of coastal Peru, dry desert conditions have helped to preserve bodies almost completely, with their hair and all the usually perishable grave offerings.

**PERUVIAN CHILD**
The body of this Peruvian child was tied to a wooden frame and left to dry in the hot, arid climate. The result was an extremely well-preserved corpse.

*Brittle, paper-like facial skin*

**LEFT HAND**
The hand from the Peruvian burial is quite well preserved, although the skin is now very hard and brittle. Study of the skin and the bones can tell us a great deal about the individual's health shortly before death.

**MUMMY BUNDLE**
This head, and its remaining hand (left) come from a sacrificial burial in Peru. Grave-goods found with the burial included a basketwork bag and a perfectly preserved stick of maize. The dry conditions have preserved the skin on most of the face.

**LEFT ARM**
This arm and hand are in an even better state of preservation than the rest of the body. The fingernails and the individual's fingerprints can be seen.

*Fingernails*

# Ancient writing

THE FIRST WRITING gradually developed in Mesopotamia (in part of modern Iraq) and was used to record trading deals. At first, pictures of the objects being exchanged were simply drawn on tokens; later, symbols were used to represent ideas. By about 3500 B.C., the actual sounds of speech (either whole words or syllables) were written down on clay tablets using a stylus. This type of script is known as cuneiform. The idea of writing spread around the Old World, and by about 1000 B.C. the Phoenicians had invented an alphabet. Writing was also independently invented in other places. In China it first appears engraved on bones to record military affairs and the deeds of kings. In Central America, the Maya used hieroglyphs, most of which have only recently been "translated," to make astronomical records and to list royal dynasties. In all these ancient societies writing was restricted to the upper classes because it was a source of knowledge and power.

**CUNEIFORM TABLET**
The earliest form of writing, known as cuneiform, consists of signs made by pressing a wedge-ended stylus into a slab of wet clay. This is an account table from Mesopotamia, dating from c. 3400 B.C.

**FOUNDATION STONE**
This four-thousand-year-old brick cone, from the famous Sumerian city of Ur, was placed in a mudbrick wall to record the foundation of a building.

*Cuneiform signs made with a wedge-ended stylus*

Seal

Impression

Seal

**CYLINDER SEAL**
This was used in early Mesopotamia to seal documents. Cylinder seals bore the name of their owner, and were simply rolled over the moist clay of a tablet to make a distinctive impression. This one is over 5,000 years old.

**BOAR SEAL** *left*
Seals were made from a variety of stones, some of them precious, and had a number of different forms. This one, dating from about 3400 B.C., takes the form of a wild boar.

Impression

**BULL SEAL** *right*
The great Indus civilization of northern India and Pakistan reached its peak between 2300 and 1750 B.C. Like the Sumerians, the Indus people also used a form of writing, and recorded trading deals with seals. This stone seal, showing a bull, is typical of the period.

Seal

Impression

Mayan writing stamped on pottery

Mayan writing engraved on bone

Painted Mayan writing

## MAYAN WRITING

For generations, scholars were baffled by the pictorial script of the Maya. It bears no resemblance to any other known writing. The first simple bars and dots of the calendar were translated in 1880, but for nearly a hundred years it was thought that Mayan writing was used only for recording the calendar and for astronomical calculations. It was not till the 1960s that researchers found that some glyphs referred to the kings and their exploits. Now nearly 80 percent are have been decoded and a history of the Maya is being uncovered.

Mayan characters

**MAYAN TOMB SLAB** *above*
The writing on this stone relief identifies it as showing the ruler "Shield Jaguar" with his wife, Lady Xoc, kneeling before him and ritually drawing blood from her tongue.

# Writing in Egypt

The idea of writing probably traveled to Egypt from western Asia, but the script itself was invented locally. Three basic kinds were used. The official script used for inscriptions was hieroglyphic; for writing on papyrus with pens, priests used a form called hieratic; a simpler kind, called demotic, was for everyday use.

**SCRIBES AT WORK** *above*
Armies of scribes were vital to the functioning of ancient Egypt's complex society. They ensured that records were kept, business conducted, and taxes collected.

**HIEROGLYPHICS** *left*
Hieroglyphic is a kind of script where the symbols stand for parts of words. It was developed about 3000 B.C. and, unlike cuneiform, was used for historical records, and on tombs and temples.

Man

Two

On

Rich

**CHINESE CHARACTERS** *above*
The Chinese script is the oldest writing still in use in the world. In the Bronze Age Shang period a form was used from around 1300 B.C. which is still recognizably related to modern Chinese. In 221 B.C. the Ch'in state brought in a standard script to replace all the regional variations that had developed, and this is still used today.

**PAPYRUS** *above*
Early paper was made from this reed.

# Bronzeworking

BRONZE IS A MIXTURE of copper and tin. Its use became widespread in Europe around 2000 B.C. Copper had been used to make metal objects before this date, but these were usually only ornamental as copper and tin are too soft to make useful tools or weapons. By adding 10 percent tin to the copper, a far harder alloy could be produced, and one which could be cast in many different shapes. It could take a sharp edge and be resharpened or melted down and recast when it was worn. These qualities made it a very useful metal. Most bronze objects (from swords to brooches, knives to pins) were made by casting - pouring the molten metal into a mold and allowing it to cool and set. Sheet-metal items such as shields were hammered into shape. While stone is abundant locally, copper ores are not common in Europe, and tin is rare, so the shift to bronze brought widespread social changes. Prospectors and miners appeared, long-distance trade in metal ingots developed, and central trading areas came into being. Control of the trade was a great source of power, and large fortified settlements grew up which dominated the trade routes and served as centers of manufacturing.

**MELTING DOWN THE ORE**
Copper and tin, the usual ingredients of bronze, occur as ores which have to be mined from the earth. In order to obtain the metal, the ore is heated to a high temperature to melt the metal and separate it from the rock. This process is known as smelting. To produce bronze, solid copper and tin ingots are melted together to form a bronze ingot. This in turn can be remelted and poured into a mold.

**A PRECIOUS METAL**
The liquid bronze was poured into the mold. The skill required to cast objects in this way, together with the specialist equipment needed, made bronze items particularly valuable. People had to be prepared to barter with the bronzeworker to obtain the things they wanted.

**BRONZE DEBRIS**
When copper and tin ores are melted together, the resulting alloy is collected in the bottom of the melting pot in bowl-shaped ingots. The debris on the left shows part of the outline of one of these.

Long blade for "slashing" action

Original golden color

## STONE MOLD

This is one section of a two-piece mold used for casting round-headed pins. When the two halves were joined together, molten bronze was poured in through holes at the pointed end of each pin. This mold is from Mörigen, Switzerland, and dates from c. 1000 B.C.

## PINS

Bronzeworkers were capable of producing quite elaborately decorated objects, as these pins from Switzerland show. The different types of patterns on pins like this can give archaeologists useful clues to the origins of bronze items and the people who made them.

## END PRODUCT

This is the type of bronze pin that would have been produced using the stone mold shown.

## READY FOR RECYCLING

These axes, dating from c. 750 B.C., are damaged. They may have formed part of the stock-in-trade of a bronzeworker, ready to melt down and recycle.

## MOMENT OF TRUTH

These bronzeworkers are casting swords whose handles are similar to to the one shown below. The person in the foreground is examining a sword to check that it is free of flaws. The mold used in this process has an extra channel to pour the metal through. When the cast had set and the mold was opened up, the excess bronze found in this channel was removed. Extra metal where the two halves of the mold joined together was also removed or smoothed down.

*Decorated hilt*

## TWO SWORDS

These swords would have been cast using the methods shown on this page. The upper sword is from Avignon, France, and the lower is from Denmark. The Danish sword has been cleaned to show its original gold color; the French sword has the dull, aged color of most ancient bronze objects.

# The beauties of bronze

BRONZE TOOLS AND WEAPONS are not much sharper than flint ones, so the original reason for developing bronzeworking around 2000 B.C. probably had to do with social status. When it is new, bronze is a shiny gold color and can be richly decorated. It soon became a valuable substance, and one which was ideally suited for showing a person's wealth and power. When it was first invented it was popular among the upper classes for ornamental objects such as jewelry. It was also used to make tools and weapons, which themselves were often impressively decorated. When iron became widespread in Europe, around 750 B.C., it was used for the heavier tools and weapons, thus freeing the bronze-workers to concentrate on producing luxury items and decorative objects, like jewelry, ornaments, and horse harness decorations.

**WHAT ARE THEY DOING?**
This mysterious engraving is taken from the design on a bronze vessel found in the Tyrol, Austria.

**PENDANT**
This beaten bronze pendant was probably suspended on a chain worn around the neck. The type of simple bronze chain in use at this time is shown on the opposite page.

*Pin is shown actual size*

*Harness mounts found in Norfolk, England*

**HORSEMANSHIP**
In the late Bronze Age the use of horses became widespread.

**TWEEZERS**
Like today, tweezers were probably used in the Bronze Age for pulling out hairs.

*Typical serpentine ornament*

*Razors were made of beaten metal, and engraved with patterns*

**RICHES OF THE CELTS**
The chariots of the aristocratic Celtic horsemen of the late Iron Age (c. 100 B.C.–A.D. 100) were decorated with fine metalwork. Here, red enamel highlights the pattern.

**BRIDLE SIDEPIECE**
This part of a horse harness was found in Cambridge, England.

**FOR USE AND ORNAMENT**
These elegant razors were found in Denmark. Human bodies, preserved in the peat in the same area, were clean shaven; people no doubt used razors similar to these.

*Bronze Age pin, fashionable after 2000 B.C.*

*Fastening held closed by tension of ring*

**SUNFLOWER PINS**
These pins are so named because of the position of their carefully crafted heads, which would have shone brightly on the clothing of the wearer. They date from c. 1200 B.C.

*Flower-shaped head*

**WORN BY THE POWERFUL**
The neck ring or "torque" was an important status symbol in the Celtic-speaking world of the Iron Age. Torques were also worn by warriors as a protective charm. This one, from the 6th century B.C., is made from a single piece of twisted bronze.

**AROUND THE WAIST**
One of a series of ornaments attached to a belt, this boss was made from a thin sheet of bronze. The decorations were hammered upward from the back, using a technique called *repoussé*. This boss is from Auvernier, Switzerland.

*Simple bent-metal link*

**SWISS JEWELRY**
This chain may have formed part of a necklace. It was found in a Bronze Age village by a Swiss lake.

**WOMEN'S BELT BOSS**
These bosses have been found with many female burials in Denmark.

**BRACELET**
Some of the richest bracelets from the Bronze Age took the form of metal spirals.

**ALL DRESSED UP**
Bronze Age women would have worn dresses like the one shown in this engraving.

Found in Denmark, this is the pattern for a woman's jacket.

# A Bronze Age warrior

THROUGHOUT THE WESTERN WORLD a more obviously warlike society was evolving around 2,200-700 B.C., the time of the Bronze Age in Europe. This period gives our first evidence of individual armed combat and of societies in which the warrior and his skills were valued. The weapons used were spears, for attacking enemies at a distance, and swords and axes, proving that hand-to-hand fighting took place. The high position of warriors during the Bronze Age is shown by the richness of their personal ornaments (which included jewelry such as bangles and pins with large ornate heads) and the elaborate decoration on some of their weapons.

**BANGLE**
This intricately engraved bangle is from Auvernier, Switzerland, and dates from c. 1200 B.C.

*Found in Switzerland, these pins date from c. 1000 B.C.*

**BEFORE BUTTONS**
Pins were used for fastening clothing before the invention of buttons.

**THE FIRST KNIGHTS**
Horseback riding became widespread in the late Bronze Age, and men used slashing swords for fighting.

**FOR FOOD OR FIGHTING?**
Small knives, like this one from Switzerland, were probably used for cutting food rather than as weapons.

**STATUS SYMBOLS**
Spears were symbols of the warrior in the Bronze Age, and were often very ornate.

**CEREMONIAL SPEARHEAD**
Together with its wooden shaft, this massive socketed spearhead from Hungary would have made a weapon over 6 ft (2m) long. It was almost certainly for ceremonial use rather than for battle.

**LIGHTWEIGHT SPEAR**
This small spear tip is from Amiens, France. The spear would have been thrown at the enemy like a javelin.

*Socket for wooden shaft*

**SHAFT-TUBE AXE**
This impressive axe from Hungary was produced as much for show as for use as a weapon. The wooden shaft was fixed in the vertical tube.

*Tube to take wooden handle*

*Socket to take long wooden handle*

**WORKING WEAPON**
Found in Hungary, this more practical decorated axe head dates from 2000-1000 B.C.

**ANTLER CHEEKPIECE**
Part of a horse's harness, the cheekpiece secures the bit in place. This example is from Corcelettes on Lake Neuchâtel, Switzerland.

*Hole for rein*

**INTO BATTLE**
A Bronze Age warrior was equipped with spears and slashing swords, like the one shown at the bottom of the page. A helmet, shield, and stout leather garments provided some protection from the enemy.

**REINING THEM IN**
This terret (loop) was attached to the pole of a cart or chariot. The reins passed through it, making for easier control by the driver. This bronze terret was found in Switzerland.

*Socket for wooden shaft*

*Swords had a sharp point, even though they were not normally used for stabbing*

**TRUSTY SWORD**
From the Bronze Age onward, the sword was the most important weapon. This sword from Denmark originally would have been kept in a leather or wooden sheath. The surface of the metal would have been a shiny gold color.

# Iron Age finery

SOME OF THE FINEST decorated personal items of the Iron Age are made of bronze, because iron was reserved for heavy tools and weapons. Unlike iron, bronze could be cast into complex shapes and be highly decorated. Classical writers report that the Celts of Iron Age Europe were fond of adornment, including body painting, elaborate hairstyles, and jewelry (pp. 34-35). A characteristic ornament was a silver neck ring called a torque (p. 45), symbolic of high social rank. Some fighting men went into battle naked except for their torque, trusting in its protective power. Over their trousers and tunics men and women wore woollen cloaks fastened with brooches, sometimes of elaborate design. In graves, it is usually only these that survive to indicate the sort of clothing that was worn. The upper classes would adorn their horses with fine harnesses covered with disks, studs, and bells.

**SPECTACLE-BROOCH**
This type of brooch is so called because of its shape. It is made from a single twisted piece of wire and would have had a pin at the back. It is from Carinthia in Austria and dates from between 1000 and 800 B.C.

*Pin*

*Spring*

**SAFETY PIN**
Brooches were the prehistoric versions of safety pins. They were used in exactly the same way as they are today, for joining clothes together. This Hungarian brooch dates from c. 50 B.C.

*Spring*

*Pin*

*Glass disk*

**A MARK OF RANK**
A composite bow made up of glass disks makes this an especially striking brooch. It would have been quite a rarity and was probably worn by someone of high rank. It is from Italy, and dates from between 800 and 700 B.C.

**CHIEFTAIN**
In this rather romantic engraving, the nineteenth-century illustrator has tried to combine all the elements known about Iron Age dress into one picture. The chieftain has a horned helmet and a bushy mustache (although pigtails are not reported!). His cloak is fastened by a brooch, and he is wearing a shiny breastplate for battle. Under his short tunic he wears trousers which are ideal for riding a horse. The woman has an elaborate girdle, from which a dagger hangs. She is presenting the chieftain with a drinking horn filled with beer taken from the decorated pail in the foreground.

**FIRM FASTENINGS**
Two more examples from northern Europe show the skill that Iron Age metalworkers could focus on these simple fasteners. The strong, sprung pins themselves are clearly visible.

**FOLLOWING THE PATTERN**
This bronze pendant with enameled decoration is from a Saxon burial slightly later than the other objects on this page. But the curves and circles used in its decoration show how this style of art continued to be used in northern Europe.

**FOR MEN AND WOMEN**
Bracelets like this were commonly worn on the arms - probably by both male and female members of the household. This one was found near Cambridge, England, and was made c. 50 B.C. Its delicate pattern would have been more striking when it was new.

**A CLEAN SHAVE**
This razor, now about 2500 years old, is less ornate than some of the razors of the Bronze Age (pp. 44-45) but it is highly functional: it would have been just as sharp as any modern straight razor. It comes from Cambridge, England.

**WELL SHOD**
Iron Age horseshoes are sometimes found. Their form is similar to those in use today.

*Decorated back of mirror*

**FAIREST OF THEM ALL**
Some of the most beautiful objects that have survived from the Iron Age are mirrors. This one is decorated in the distinctive, swirling style of Celtic art. The back is shown in the photograph; the other side would be highly polished to give a reflection. Mirrors like this are rare and no doubt belonged to the wealthiest families.

**BOAR HUNT**
Iron horseshoes similar to the one above can be seen in this old engraving. The fine trappings that decorate the horses of the huntsmen are also clearly shown. The large disks are made of bronze and are known as phalerae. In the Iron Age the boar was hunted for sport as well as for its meat.

# Life in the Iron Age

**INSTANT PATTERNS**
Later Saxon potters made similar shaped pots to those of the Iron Age, but decorated them with punches.

Punch for cross pattern

Punch for circle pattern

THE FIRST REALLY SKILLED IRONWORKERS were the Hittites, who lived in what is now central Turkey. They perfected the techniques of smelting ore and making iron objects around 1500 B.C. The Hittites guarded the secrets of ironworking carefully, but when their empire was overthrown their knowledge spread across Europe, where the Iron Age began around 1100 B.C. By this time, Europe was quite densely settled with small farming communities. Although the society as a whole was ruled by a warrior class (pp. 52-53), life for the majority of people consisted of an unending round of farming activities, basically unchanged for generations. Settlements were still mainly family-based, and even small children played a full part in daily work. Many iron objects (especially tools) have survived from this period, as well as a large amount of pottery, and decorative objects made of bronze.

**BOG PEOPLE**
Bodies preserved in the airless conditions of European peat bogs give us a glimpse of the actual people of the Iron Age. Tollund Man, discovered in Denmark, dates from about 210 B.C.

**BRONZE BOWL**
In the Iron Age many of the more decorative and high-status objects were in fact made of bronze, a material that looked shiny and could be engraved with detailed patterns. Fine bronze imported tableware like this bowl was highly prized by many upper-class families in northern Europe, who were eager to adopt Mediterranean customs.

*Engraved decoration*

*Shape made by hammering out bronze*

**STATUS SYMBOL?**
In the last hundred years before the Roman invasion of Britain, wealthy people developed a taste for fine pottery. Beakers like this one were imported from Europe in large numbers.

This smaller decorated pot was found in a British Iron Age burial mound.

### IRON TOOLS
The introduction of iron into Europe provided an ideal material for making sturdy tools and weapons; iron was also more widely available than the tin and copper needed to make bronze. Unfortunately, iron corrodes (rots away) much more quickly than bronze, so most of the items that have survived are in poorer condition than bronze objects of the same period.

### KNIFE
This small iron-bladed knife has a handle made of antler. Although the blade is corroded, the handle is very well preserved because of favorable soil conditions.

*Iron blade*

*Antler handle*

*Iron blade*

*Iron blade*

*Antler handle*

### HARVESTER
This reaping hook has the same sickle-shaped design that was used for gathering hay or crops throughout the prehistoric period (pp. 30-31). This example has an antler handle.

*Serrated (notched) cutting edge*

*Holes for attaching wooden handle*

### CUTTER
A wooden handle made this iron saw almost as easy to use as its modern counterpart.

### FORGING AHEAD
In this old engraving of blacksmiths at work, the method of shaping a piece of hot metal by hammering it is clearly shown. In the background, more iron is being heated in a furnace.

### TONGS
Iron was worked by beating it into shape while it was red hot. The metal was held in large tongs, like these from Norfolk, England.

# Men of iron

WE KNOW ABOUT the Celtic-speaking peoples who lived north of the Alps from about 500 B.C. through the reports of Greek and Roman historians. They describe barbarian people with customs quite different from their own, such as human sacrifice and head-hunting. These tribes were ruled by warriors, who placed a high value on their heroic lifestyle, which included feasting and drinking, reciting poetry, singing, horseback riding, and, of course, skill in battle. The Celts were as concerned with scaring their enemies as with actually fighting them. We know this because of the fearsome appearance of their arms, armor, and other possessions.

**LANCE HEAD**
This unusually shaped object is made of wrought iron.

*Human head*

**HEAD IN HAND**
The handle of this dagger is shaped like a human figure. It dates from 100 B.C.-A.D. 100.

**LETHAL LONDONER**
This is a fine early dagger from c. 500 B.C., found in the Thames River, London.

**SHINY SHEATH**
Made from thin sheets of bronze riveted together, this sheath has a birch-bark lining.

A nineteenth-century illustration of a Celtic warrior chief in battle

**HELMET FOR A HERO**
This bronze helmet would have belonged to a high-ranking warrior, and was probably for display rather than battle.

*Hollow horn made of riveted sheet bronze*

19th-century illustration of Iron Age warfare

*Oak lining*

*Diameter of tankard is about 7 in (175 mm)*

*Loops for fastening leather interior*

**AXLE HUB**
This decoration was attached to the axle of a light chariot of the type used against the Roman army invading Britain.

**WHAT YOUR RIGHT ARM IS FOR...**
Drinking was popular with the warriors, as this 4 pint (2.3 liter) bronze vessel shows. The drink was probably a beer made from barley.

**BRONZE TERRET**
This was fixed to the yoke of a chariot (p. 47).

**BIT BETWEEN THE TEETH**
The bit is inserted in the horse's mouth and controlled by pulling on the reins. It has an iron core covered with decorated bronze.

**IRON SWORD** *below*
This sword would have had a decorated sheath of leather or wood. It dates from c. 150 B.C.-A.D. 50.

*Hilt (handle) would have been covered in wood, bone, or leather*

# Ancient China

FOR THOUSANDS OF YEARS, Chinese civilization evolved with little or no contact with the Western world, and the Chinese made several independent inventions, such as farming and writing. The first stone-using agricultural communities were followed by a variety of societies, most of which survived by farming a range of crops including rice and millet. True civilization dates from c. 1500 B.C. with the Bronze Age Shang Dynasty. At this time China was a loose group of states which were gradually joined together. Between 500 and 200 B.C., the two principal states, Ch'u and Ch'in, battled for power. Under the victorious Ch'in and the later Han (206 B.C.-A.D. 220) an empire of 60 million people prospered. The Great Wall was built, and standard systems of writing, laws, and taxes were created.

**RARE AND DEADLY** *above*
The halberd is a weapon mounted at right-angles on a tall wooden shaft, kind of like a 15th century pike. This halberd of white jade is over 3,000 years old. It was probably both for battle and for ceremonial use, especially for sacrifices.

**CHINESE NOBLEMEN**
These men belonged to the court of Emperor Tscheu-Sin, c. 1150 B.C.

**RITUAL HALBERD**
This sacrificial halberd is a good example of the superb bronzeworking of the Shang Dynasty (1523-1027 B.C.). This skill arose from local roots, although there was also some outside influence from the West. With its ornate patterns, this halberd would have played an important role in rituals, for both human and animal sacrifices.

**STONE TOOLS**
Like their counterparts in Europe, the first Chinese farmers had to clear forests with stone axes and till the soil with mattocks (pickaxes). Both of these tools have similar shapes the world over. In China, however, they were used to cultivate different crops - millet in the north and rice in the south.

Stone mattock

Polished stone axe from Shansi, northern China

**BRONZE AXE**
This is the head of a ritual axe known as a *yüeh*, which was used for beheading humans at sacrifices made at funerals. These axes are often very highly decorated. The holes make the head easier to bind to the wooden shaft.

**BRONZE HALBERD BLADE**
The halberd was the chief weapon in ancient Chinese society. This rather simple example was used for combat. Like the other bronze halberds shown here, this one comes from the Shang dynasty (16th to 11th centuries B.C.).

*Cutting edge*

*Cutting edge*

**THE GREAT WALL**
Built between about 350 and 200 B.C., the Great Wall stretches for over 2,500 miles along China's northern frontier. An army of laborers was used to build the wall, which was meant to keep out nomads from Mongolia.

**TERRACOTTA WARRIOR**
From 246-210 B.C., over 700,000 workers labored over the tomb of one of China's greatest emperors, Qin Shi Huang Di. It is guarded by an army of over 7,500 terracotta warriors such as this, each one different.

# Small change

**GOD OF RICHES**
This relief shows the goddess Demeter and her son Plutus, the god of riches in Greek mythology.

We usually think of money as consisting of coins and bank notes, but anything used when making payments can be called money. In ancient societies many different things, from small shells to huge stones punched with holes, have been used to make payments, and some of these types of currency are still used today. The most common way of making a payment was originally barter, in which one item was exchanged for another. For many societies without currency, gift-giving was very important and some valued objects were regularly passed around as gifts. Other large or rare forms of money, such as cattle or perforated stones, might be given for payments of a social kind, such as compensation for a person killed, or in exchange for a woman taken as a bride. Even after standard coinage was developed about 2,500 years ago, this social use of money continued; many examples shown here come from recent societies.

Rice

**TRADE IN RICE**
As well as using coinage, the Chinese used food, especially rice, to pay for different kinds of goods.

**CHINESE CURRENCY**
In China, coinage was invented quite independently of the Western world, but later, in the fifth century B.C. The first coins looked like tiny knives; later ones were round.

*Knife shape is common in early Chinese currency*

**DOGS' TEETH**
This necklace from Papua New Guinea is made up of the canine teeth of dogs, threaded on to a leather thong. Its function was the same as the larger one from Africa (above right).

**FOR CARRYING CASH**
Cowrie shells have been used as money since prehistoric times. This wickerwork purse for carrying them comes from the Congo, central Africa.

**STONE NECKLACE**
This is not simply an item of personal jewelry: the beads were also used to make payments. This necklace, from Ghana (Africa), is made of perforated quartz pebbles.

*Quartz pebbles*

**GAMBLING COUNTERS**
Gambling is as old as money itself, and so gambling counters have a long history. These decorated porcelain counters are from Hong Kong and are nearly 2,000 years old.

Cowrie shells from India

*Disk is about 9 in (23 cm) in diameter*

*Stone is about 2 ft (60 cm) in diameter. The largest were up to 13 ft (4 m) across.*

**TOO BIG FOR THE POCKET**
In the Naya hills of Tibet, high up in the Himalayas, metal disks like this were used as currency. Known as *laya*, this particular example is rather small, and had half the value of the more usual large size

**MONEY STONE**
From Yap Island, north of New Guinea, limestone disks known as *fei* were used as currency.

**GREEK COIN**
This coin is from Aegina, Greece. The turtle is the symbol of the city.

# Central Americans

P<small>EOPLE FIRST CAME TO AMERICA</small> about 15,000 years ago, when hunters from Siberia followed big game across the land bridge to Alaska. These people soon began to move south and to develop without contact with the Old World. By 6000 B.C. corn was being grown in Central America (in Mexico, Guatemala, El Salvador, and Belize), and gradually a number of spectacular civilizations developed. These had large ceremonial centers with temples, palaces, and markets. Many practiced a ritual ball game in specially laid-out courts. Some had an elaborate religion that included human sacrifice, and used a kind of picture-writing that is only just being understood. These civilizations were at their height between A.D. 300-900, after which they collapsed. They were followed by a succession of empires, such as the Aztec, the one found and overthrown by the Spanish in 1519.

**WHISTLE**
This whistle is made of pottery. It comes from Guatemala and is thought to represent a stylized bird.

**POTTERY**
This piece of decorated pottery, dating to around A.D. 500, comes from Teotihuacán, at the time the largest city in Mexico.

**CALENDAR STONE**
The calendar was of great importance in the daily life of the Aztecs. Each day had its own good or evil tidings, and each month its special ceremonies. There were two different years, of 260 and 365 days, both based on a 20-day cycle.

**STONE HEAD**
From Seibal in Guatemala, this sandstone head may have decorated a temple. It dates from the Classic period, A.D. 300-900.

**TEMPLE CARVINGS**
This is a typical example of Classic period temple sculpture, showing animals, people, symbolic twisted serpents, and images of gods. It comes from a temple at Xochicalco.

**FUNERARY URN** *right*
In the Oaxaca Valley of Mexico, the Monte Albán civilization flourished from A.D. 300-900. The dead were buried in tombs with brightly painted walls. Inside the tomb, their ashes would be housed in pottery urns such as this one. It represents a god sitting cross-legged, with an elaborate headdress containing the symbol by which he is known.

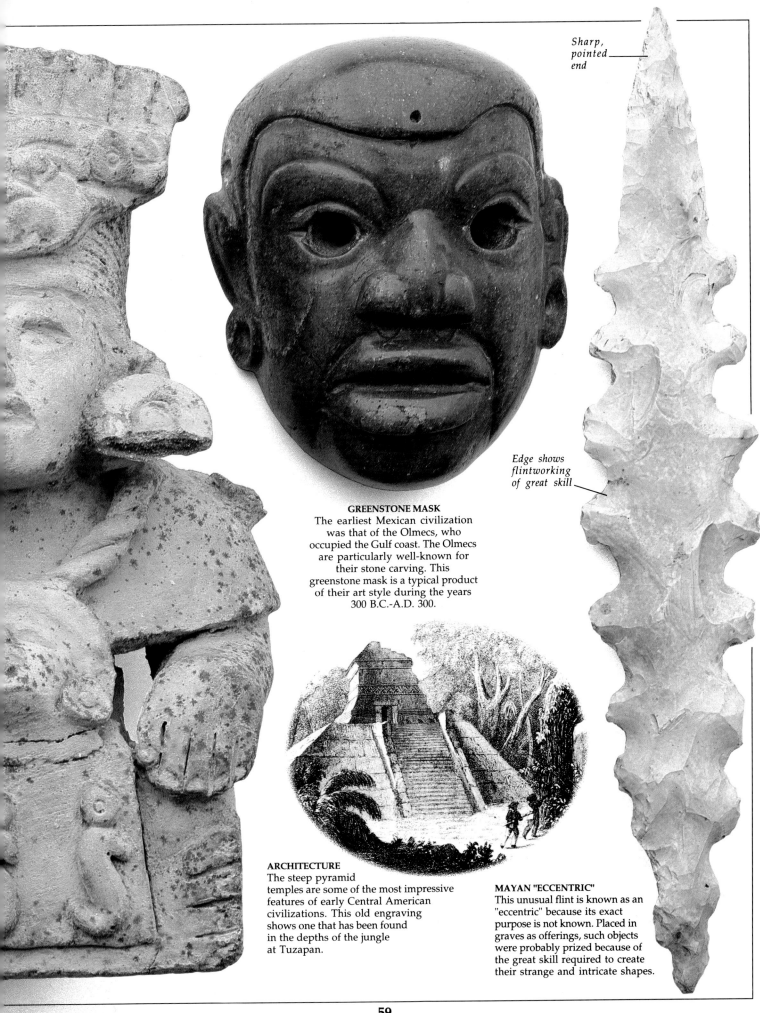

_Sharp,
pointed
end_

**GREENSTONE MASK**
The earliest Mexican civilization
was that of the Olmecs, who
occupied the Gulf coast. The Olmecs
are particularly well-known for
their stone carving. This
greenstone mask is a typical product
of their art style during the years
300 B.C.-A.D. 300.

_Edge shows
flintworking
of great skill_

**ARCHITECTURE**
The steep pyramid
temples are some of the most impressive
features of early Central American
civilizations. This old engraving
shows one that has been found
in the depths of the jungle
at Tuzapan.

**MAYAN "ECCENTRIC"**
This unusual flint is known as an
"eccentric" because its exact
purpose is not known. Placed in
graves as offerings, such objects
were probably prized because of
the great skill required to create
their strange and intricate shapes.

# North Americans

**STONE DAGGER BLADE**
Before the Europeans arrived, all native American tools and weapons were made of stone. The men used daggers like this one for fighting and as a status symbol.

**INDIAN WARFARE**
Warfare formed an important part of the life of the Plains Indians.

SINCE THE TIME OF COLUMBUS, Europeans have called the original inhabitants of North America "Indians." This is misleading, since these people had no national identity. They lived in areas as diverse as the Arctic and the deserts of the southwest, and differed in their lifestyles. In the north, the Cree hunted moose and caribou. In the northeast, tribes such as the Huron and the Iroquois relied more on agriculture. Those in the northwest were mainly fishermen; the Apache were hunters and farmers in the southwest. Most of the objects here come from the tribes of the great central plains. Before the Europeans arrived they cultivated the fertile lands along rivers and streams and hunted buffalo during the summer. After European contact they took easily to horses and used them to help in their hunting. The huge herds of buffalo then played a greater role in the lives of the Plains Indians - they could eat the meat, make the hides into clothes and wigwams, and use the bones and horns to make tools. Although they have survived attempts by white settlers to wipe them out, few native Americans now follow a traditional lifestyle.

**MEN'S MOCCASINS**
These stitched leather shoes were perhaps the most typical item of native American clothing. As with other garments, they were often highly decorated. This pair, from the Blackfoot tribe, are covered in blue beads.

*Beads*

*Leather thongs*

*Fur*

**THE PLAINS COMMUNITY**
While the men hunted, the Plains Indian women stayed in the temporary wigwam camps. They prepared food, carried out domestic tasks such as weaving, and raised the children.

**CHIEF'S HEADDRESS**
Yellow Calf, the last chief of the Arapaho tribe of Plains Indians, was the owner of this headdress. It is decorated with fur and feathers.

**SCRAPING TOOL**
Hides were prepared
by scraping them
with a metal-bladed,
bone-handled tool.
Earlier peoples used
flints in a similar way.

*Horsehair*

**PAINTED HIDE**
This animal hide is
decorated with colored ink
drawings of warriors mounted on
horseback attacking bowmen with
spears. The horsemen are wearing
long feather headdresses. This
hide is about 6 ft (2 m) long. It
belonged to a group of Sioux or Crow
Indians.

*Feathers indicate
success in hunting
and war*

**EARTH LODGE**
Some tribes built their homes by
constructing a roof over a deep
pit. This illustration shows
such a dwelling - a Mandan
earth lodge - in the nine-
teenth century.

# Digging up the past

ARCHAEOLOGY PROVIDES our only means of studying most early people, as written records have only been available for a fraction of our time on earth. Modern archaeology is a far cry from its old image of hunting for treasure in lost cities. Today the archaeologist employs a whole battery of scientific techniques to help detect, excavate, and analyze the remains of ancient societies. He or she is most likely to be interested in small pieces of pottery or fragments of insects, plants, or animals, because of the information these can give about everyday life. Although archaeology is often thought of as excavation, the story only begins there. Once a "dig" is over a great deal of time is spent analyzing the material recovered, and preparing it for publication. When it is published, the notes, finds, and samples are displayed or stored in a museum.

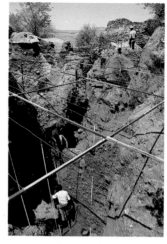

**WORKING ON SITE**
Unlike the careless treasure hunting of the past, modern excavation stresses the accurate vertical and horizontal recording of all features of a site. This is the excavation of an early hominid site at Sterkfontein, South Africa.

**PHOTOGRAPHIC SCALES**
Photographs form a vital part of the records of an excavation. These scales are essential for judging the size of the subject being photographed.

**CAST OF THOUSANDS**
Giovanni Belzoni was one of the first to bring Egyptian relics to the West. However, he was a shameless treasure hunter who also destroyed much important material.

Trowel

*Small, solid-forged steel blade*

Paintbrush

Toothbrush

Cotton gloves

**CLEANING**
For items needing careful cleaning on site, a variety of instruments, such as these brushes, might be used.

Metric scales

**TROWEL AND GLOVES**
The trowel is the main tool used for excavation. Gloves may be used to handle delicate finds after digging.

Individual pins
trace out shape
of object

R4F4, 27, STON, FLAK, , 8140683 &GD,
blh.rf.dat: RSFS, 28, STON, FLAK,
blh.rf.dat: RSFS, 42, STON, FLAK,
bop.rf.dat: RSFS, 43, STON, FLAK,
bop.rf.dat: TIF4, 19, STON, FLAK,
bop.rf.dat: 0.64, STON, FLAK,
bop.rf.dat: 1193, 21, STON, FLAK,
bop.rf.dat: 1016, 22, STON, FLAK,
bop.rf.dat: 16, 650, STON, FLAK,
bop.rf.dat: 287, 26, STON, FLAK,
bop.rf.dat: 297, 648, STON, FLAK,
bop.rf.dat: 307, 649, STON, FLAK,
bop.rf.dat: 311, 25, STON, FLAK,
bop.rf.dat: 311, 647, STON, FLAK,
bop.rf.dat: 313, 23, STON, FLAK,
bop.rf.dat: 313, 24, STON, FLAK,
bop.rf.dat: 313, 30, STON, FLAK,
bop.rf.dat: 313, 31, STON, FLAK,
bop.rf.dat: 313, 32, STON, FLAK,
bop.rf.dat: 313, 33, STON, FLAK,
bop.rf.dat: 313, 36, STON, FLAK,
bop.rf.dat: 313, 37, STON, FLAK,
bop.rf.dat: 313, 39, STON, FLAK,
bop.rf.dat: 313, 40, STON, FLAK,
bop.rf.dat: 313, 641, STON, FLAK,
bop.rf.dat: 313, 642, STON, FLAK,
bop.rf.dat: 313, 643, STON, FLAK,
bop.rf.dat: 313, 644, STON, FLAK,
bop.rf.dat: 313, 645, STON, FLAK,
bop.rf.dat: 313, 646, STON, FLAK,
bop.rf.dat: 328, 639, STON, FLAK,
bop.rf.dat: 329, 638, STON, FLAK,
bop.rf.dat: 387, 68, STON, FLAK,
bop.rf.dat: 387, 70, STON, FLAK,
bop.rf.dat: 430, 632, STON, FLAK,
bop.rf.dat: 446, 73, STON, FLAK,
bop.rf.dat: 600, 71, STON, FLAK

**INDEX CARDS**
These can be used to
record all finds.

Potsherd

**COMPUTER
PRINTOUT**
Most excavations now
produce such a huge mass
of data that computers
offer the best way to
analyze it.

Drawing pens

**SIZE AND SHAPE**
An important part of the post-
excavation process is the
recording and dating of the
finds, such as this sherd of
pottery. A profile gauge can be
used to trace the outlines of curved
or irregularly shaped items.

**CALIPERS**
These are for
measuring the
dimensions of finds
that have
awkward shapes
and thicknesses.

Colored pencils

Label for recording
details and setting
in which find was
recovered

**BAGGING A FIND**
All individual finds and samples are
kept in separate plastic bags. The
label records the site name and the
exact setting of the find.

**THE DISCOVERER OF TROY**
Heinrich Schliemann (1822-90) set
out to prove that the Troy of Homer's
legends was a real place. He did so, but
his excavation methods were careless.
He actually dug straight through the
levels he was looking for into remains
of an older period.

**SITE DIAGRAM**
All excavated features are
recorded on site by making scale
drawings in pencil on waterproof
scaled paper. After the dig is over,
these will be redrawn in ink and
perhaps color-coded in preparation
for publication.

**MEASUREMENT**
Precise measurement is essential in archaeology.
Here, an anthropologist is measuring a skull
fragment from an early hominid called *Australopithecus boisei*. Tiny differences in skull shape can
show where it fits in the evolutionary pattern.

**TAPE MEASURE**
The tape measure is just one of the many
measuring devices used in modern archaeology.

# Index

# Acknowledgments

**Dorling Kindersley would like to thank:**
Peter Bailey and Lester Cheeseman for additional design assistance; Angela Murphy for additional picture research; Dr Schuyler Jones, Julia Cousins, Ray Inskeep, John Todd and John Simmonds of the Pitt-Rivers Museum, Oxford; Dr David Phillipson of the University Museum of Archaeology and Anthropology, Cambridge; Gavin Morgan of the Museum of London; Colin Keates and Chris Stringer of the Natural History Museum; the staff of the Museum of Mankind; Dave King and Jonathan Buckley. Meryl Silbert.

**The following museums provided objects for photography**
British Museum (Natural History), 6-7, 10-11, 14-15, 18-19, 22-3
Museum of London, 26-7, 30-1, 32-3, 46-7, 52-3, 62-3
Museum of Mankind, 20-1, 38-9, 60-1
Pitt-Rivers Museum, Oxford, 12-13, 16-17, 28-9, 34-5, 36-7, 56-7
University Museum of Archaeology and Anthropology, Cambridge, 24-5, 40-1, 42-3, 44-5, 48-9, 50-1, 54-5, 58-9

**Picture credits**
t=top, b=bottom, c=center, l=left, r=right

Angela Murphy 7bl, 23cl
Bridgeman Art Library 62lc
British Museum (Natural History) 6r, 15bl, 19bc
Bruce Coleman 7bc, 10l, 62tr, 63br
Mansell Collection 8cl, 9br, 13c, 17tr, 27bc, 33tl, 36tc, 36lc, 38c, 41rc, 42tl, 43rc, 46lc
Mary Evans Picture Library 9tr, 16tl, 20tr, 21bc, 22br, 25br, 26tl, 30lc, 31br, 32br, 35c, 41tr, 42c, 51br, 52rc, 53tl, 54c
Museum of London 24bc, 25tl, 47c, 48bl
Peter Newark's Historical Pictures 24tl, 25cl, 28tc, 34tl, 41bc, 49br, 60tl, 60br, 61br
Ronald Sheridan's Photo-Library 22tr, 38tl, 50tl, 55r 63br
Topham Picture Library 10bl

**Illustrators**
John Woodcock
John James
Mark Bergin